THE EVERYTHING KIDS' RACECARS PUZZLE AND ACTIVITY BOOK

Put the pedal to the metal for laps and laps of fun!

Beth L. Blair and Jennifer A. Ericsson

adamsmedia
Avon, Massachusetts

EDITORIAL
Director of Innovation: Paula Munier
Editorial Director: Laura M. Daly
Associate Copy Chief: Sheila Zwiebel
Acquisitions Editor: Kerry Smith
Production Editor: Casey Ebert

PRODUCTION
Director of Manufacturing: Susan Beale
Production Project Manager: Michelle Roy Kelly
Prepress: Erick DaCosta, Matt LeBlanc
Managing Designer: Heather Blank
Interior Layout: Heather Barrett,
Brewster Brownville, Colleen Cunningham,
Jennifer Oliveira

An Everything® Series Book.
Everything® and everything.com® are registered trademarks of F+W Publications, Inc.

Published by Adams Media, an F+W Publications Company
57 Littlefield Street, Avon, MA 02322. U.S.A.
www.adamsmedia.com

ISBN-10: 1-59869-243-7
ISBN-13: 978-1-59869-243-3

Printed in the United States of America.

J I H G F E D C B A

This publication is designed to provide accurate and authoritative information with regard to the subject
matter covered. It is sold with the understanding that the publisher is not engaged in rendering legal,
accounting, or other professional advice. If legal advice or other expert assistance is required, the ser-
vices of a competent professional person should be sought.
—From a *Declaration of Principles* jointly adopted by a Committee of the
American Bar Association and a Committee of Publishers and Associations

Many of the designations used by manufacturers and sellers to distinguish their products are claimed as
trademarks. When those designations appear in this book and Adams Media was aware of a trademark
claim, the designations have been printed with initial capital letters.

Cover illustrations by Dana Regan.
Interior illustrations by Kurt Dolber.
Puzzles by Beth L. Blair.

This book is available at quantity discounts for bulk purchases.
For information, please call 1-800-289-0963.

See the entire Everything® series at *www.everything.com*.

CONTENTS

DEDICATION

To GeeP and RPM, my favorite racing fans! Love, Aunt Beth

To Anthony and Austin.
Love, Aunt Jenny

INTRODUCTION

Does the thought of brightly painted cars speeding around a track make your heart pound and your blood race? Do you have posters of Dale Earnhardt, Michael Schumacher, Danica Patrick, or Jeff Gordon hanging on the walls of your bedroom? Do words like *cylinder*, *crankshaft*, and *throttle* get you all pumped up? Do you own a personal set of earplugs? Then you must be a racecar fan!

If that's true, *The Everything® Kids' Racecars Puzzle and Activity Book* will be just what you need to keep you in a racing mood! Included in this book are nine chapters stuffed full of puzzles on all types of racing. We've covered everything from the beginnings of the sport to the cutting-edge technology of today and tomorrow! Some chapters focus on the nuts and bolts of the cars, others on talented drivers and enthusiastic fans like you! We showcase record-breaking events and crashes, and even offer you do-it-yourself racing ideas. As you race your way through the book, don't be surprised if you learn some amazing things about your favorite sport and the super cars that make it so popular. For instance, did you know that inside the engine of a speeding Formula One car, the piston can travel up and down 300 times a second?!

Just as people like different types of racing, people like different types of puzzles. We've included a variety to please all puzzlers. You'll find word searches, codes, math puzzles, mazes, rebuses, crisscrosses, acrostics, and more. There are also racing games and other activities for you to try!

To give you a little sample of what you can expect, see how quickly you can solve this Racecar Palindrome Maze.

What's a palindrome, you ask? It's a word that reads the same both forward and backward—like the word *racecar*. Take a practice lap by seeing how quickly you can go forward and back again through the word—without crossing your own path!

All warmed up? What are you waiting for? Start your engines, grab a pencil, and zoom into the rest of the puzzles!

Beth L. "Speedster" Blair

Jennifer A. "Hot Rod" Ericsson

Number One

One of the first auto races was held in 1887. But before the race ever started, it was cancelled! To find out why, cross out cars with letter pairs that have an I, F, or T. Read the remaining cars from left to right and top to bottom.

START ► 9 + 13 + 14 + 8 − 9 +

12 − 3 ÷ 4 + 10 + 4 −

2 × 10 ÷ 2 × 10 × 2 ×

6 − 3 + 15 × 3 ÷ 9 + 10 ÷ 2

Slow and Steady

In 1894, twenty-one cars entered a race in France. Judges weren't looking to see who could go the fastest. They wanted to know which car was the most "safe and economical"! Good thing, because the top speeds in this race will surprise you.

To see how fast these first "race" cars went, complete the equation that runs around the page. Write your answer in the shaded box.

miles per hour

Chop Shop

This classic racecar has been put in a grid and chopped into twelve pieces. How quickly can you copy the pattern in each square into the numbered grid to put this car back together again?

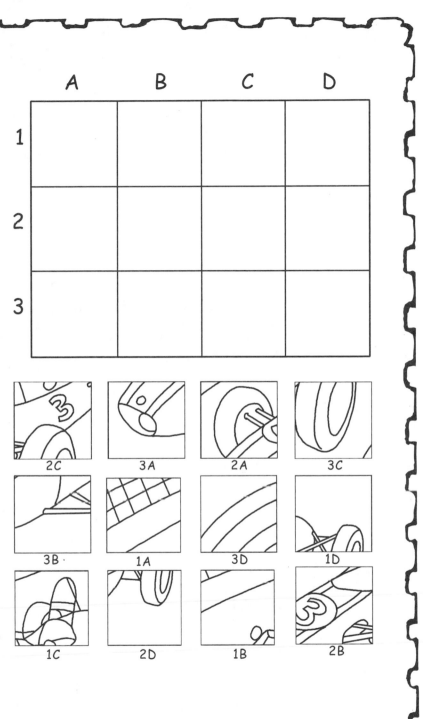

	A	B	C	D
1				
2				
3				

2C 3A 2A 3C

3B 1A 3D 1D

1C 2D 1B 2B

Muscle Car

At first, racecars were made for two passengers—the driver and a mechanic. Not only could the mechanic make repairs during a race, he was useful in unexpected ways. In 1912, Ralph DePalma sure needed his mechanic's help to get across the finish line. Connect the dots to find out how these guys managed to stay in eleventh place after their car broke down!

Big Changes

In the 1970s there were two things that changed the sport of car racing forever. To see what they were, figure out which letters are described by each fraction. Print the letters, in order, from left to right in the boxes provided.

Can you spot five differences between these two vintage racecars?

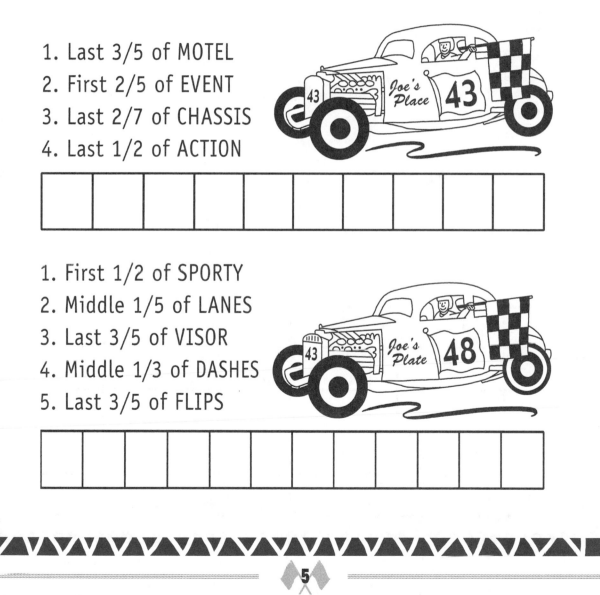

1. Last 3/5 of MOTEL
2. First 2/5 of EVENT
3. Last 2/7 of CHASSIS
4. Last 1/2 of ACTION

1. First 1/2 of SPORTY
2. Middle 1/5 of LANES
3. Last 3/5 of VISOR
4. Middle 1/3 of DASHES
5. Last 3/5 of FLIPS

Down and Dirty

The first racetracks weren't the smooth black ovals of today. They were just dirt. This sure made for a rough and bumpy ride! Find the one path that goes from START to FINISH, missing the bumps and ruts along the way!

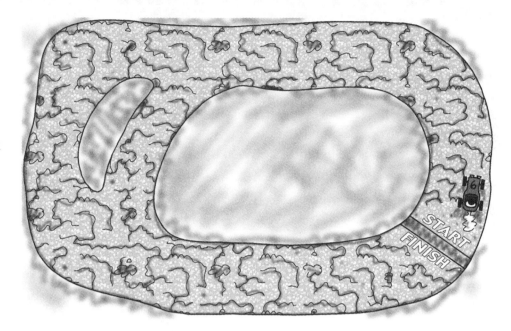

Racing Is Born

In what country was automobile racing started in the 1800s? To find out, fill in all the spaces that have a dot in the center.

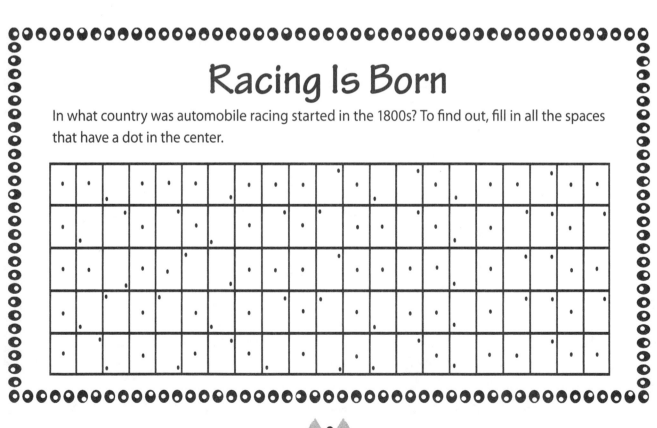

Silly Speedster

Each definition below suggests a word. Write the word on the dotted lines, and then put each letter in its proper place in the grid. The first one has been done for you. Work back and forth between the grid and the answers until you can read the silly answer to the riddle.

A. Light brown

T̲ A̲ N̲
2 29 13

B. Number after two

‾26 ‾16 ‾28 ‾4 ‾33

C. Clothing for hands

‾8 ‾32 ‾24 ‾5 ‾19 ‾11

D. Small shack

‾23 ‾25 ‾30

E. To carry or haul

‾31 ‾9 ‾22 ‾17

F. What we breathe

‾12 ‾21 ‾7

G. Drink from grapes

‾20 ‾1 ‾3 ‾10

H. Very tired

‾15 ‾6 ‾27 ‾18 ‾14

WHY IS AN OLD RACE CAR LIKE A BABY?

1G	2A T		3G	4B	5C	6H	7F
		8C	9E	10G	11C		
12F	13A N	14H	15H	16B	17E	18H	19C
20G	21F	22E	23D	24C	25D	26B	
27H		28B	29A A	30D	31E	32C	33B

Making Fast Cars

During the first years of track racing, manufacturers kept adding special features to their cars, trying to make them faster than all the rest. To learn the first racecar brand names, follow the directions to add letters to each word below. Add letters in order from left to right. Many of these companies still make cars today. How many names do you recognize?

Add the opposite of stop — P E U _ E _ T

Add quadruple Es and a Z — M _ R C _ D _ S - B _ N _

Add a large rodent — _ E N _ U L _

Add the last two letters of HAT — F I _ _

Add a place for cows — A L _ _ _ O _ E O

Add a place to sit — M A _ S _ R _ _ I

Add an insect — _ _ _ A T T I

Add money to join a group — _ _ _ _ _ E N B E R G

Add not feeling well — M _ _ _ E R

Add how old you are — D E L _ _ _

Add a delivery truck — _ _ _ W A L L

Add what you hear with — F _ R R _ _ I

Add a policeman — _ O _ _ E R

Add you and me — L O T _ _

Add a female horse — _ C L _ _ _ N

Add a writing tool — _ _ _ S K E

That's a Race?

The first auto race of any kind in the United States took place in Chicago in November, 1895. The winner, Frank Duryea, had to face some challenges that modern-day racecar drivers can't even imagine. Break each code to learn what they were. You'll be amazed!

First-to-Last Code

mpireU asw equiredr ot ider ni arc ot reventp heatingc.

Vowel Scramble Code

Uvaruga spaad wus jost ivar savan melas par hior.

Letter Switch Code
(A = B, B = C, C = D, etc.)

Hs snnj lnqd sgzm sdm gntqr sn sqzudk 54 lhkdr.

AEIOU / 1 2 3 4 5 Code

W13t2d f4r f45r m3n5t2s 1t 1 r13lr41d cr4ss3ng f4r tr13n t4 p1ss.

I hate it when this happens!

Reverse Word Code

daH ot dnif htimskcalb pohs ot riaper nekorb gnireets mra.

Zap

At this first race, drivers wore suits and hats, the track was dirt, and most people in the crowd drove a horse and buggy. But there was one thing that seemed strangely modern: The winning car used a fuel that cars are just beginning to use today! Break the code to learn what it was.

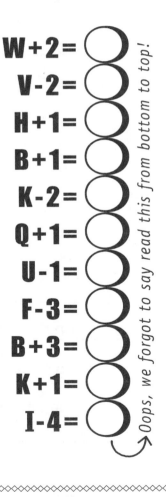

W + 2 = ◯
V - 2 = ◯
H + 1 = ◯
B + 1 = ◯
K - 2 = ◯
Q + 1 = ◯
U - 1 = ◯
F - 3 = ◯
B + 3 = ◯
K + 1 = ◯
I - 4 = ◯

↳ *Oops, we forgot to say read this from bottom to top!*

RACE	NOW	RUSH	DART	GO
IF	SPEED	YOU	FLY	DASH
HURRY	RUN	ZIP	SPRINT	CAN

Try Hard

The first "modern" car race (on a closed, oval track) in the United States was held in Rhode Island in 1896. Fifty thousand people showed up to watch seven cars motor around the Narragansett Park Speedway. It was easy to see that folks weren't too sure about these strange new racecars!

To see what the starter yelled to begin the race, cross out all the words that mean HURRY UP. Read the remaining five words from left to right and top to bottom.

Mad Dash

Some early racecar drivers got their start carrying illegal liquor in the 1920s when buying and drinking alcohol was forbidden in the United States. These drivers modified their cars to make them faster than the police cars that were chasing them! To find two common names for this high-speed activity, cross out all of the D-A-S-Hs on these curvy mountain roads. Read the remaining letters from top to bottom.

Founding Father

One man, William France, Sr., thought there should be a national organization that would govern stock car racing in the United States. He wanted to see standard rules and regulations for all races! After much hard work, he formed a group in Daytona Beach, Florida, in 1948. Use the racecar decoder to learn what familiar organization this determined man created.

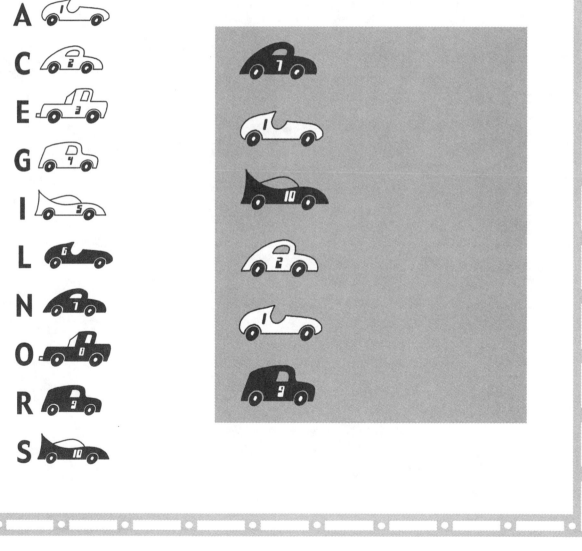

Fully Equipped

Stock cars are modeled after passenger cars, but because they are built for racing they have many special features. See if you can find all of these racecar parts hidden in this car. Use a highlight marker to run a single line of color through each word as you find it. When you are through, look at the crazy racing stripes this car will have!

kill switch   sway bar   TV camera   big engines
firewall   spoiler   no muffler
smooth tires   roll cage
fuel cell
data recorder

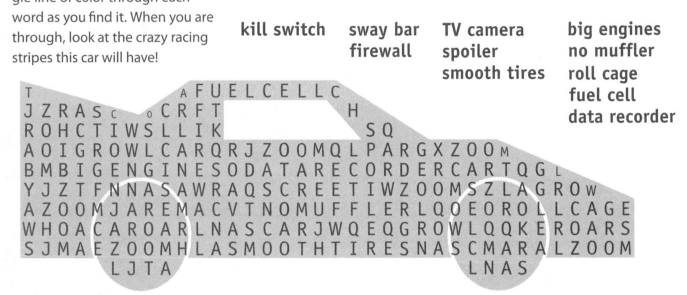

```
T              A F U E L C E L L C
J Z R A S  C   O C R F T              H
R O H C T I W S L L I K            S Q
A O I G R O W L C A R Q R J Z O O M Q L P A R G X Z O O M
B M B I G E N G I N E S O D A T A R E C O R D E R C A R T Q G L
Y J Z T F N N A S A W R A Q S C R E E T I W Z O O M S Z L A G R O W
A Z O O M J A R E M A C V T N O M U F F L E R L Q O E O R O L L C A G E
W H O A C A R O A R L N A S C A R J W Q E Q G R O W L Q Q K E R O A R S
S J M A E Z O O M H L A S M O O T H T I R E S N A S C M A R A L Z O O M
        L J T A                              L N A S
```

OIL CHANGE

Although oil changes are not done during pit stops, it is important maintenance for racecar engines! NASCAR crews change the oil after each race. Change the same letter in each pair of these O-I-L words to form two brand new words.

COIL and TOIL *(change the I to __)* **CO_L and TO_L**

BOIL and SOIL *(change the O to __)* **B_IL and S_IL**

FOIL and COIL *(change the I to __)* **FO_L and CO_L**

Bye Bye

A "top fuel" car, or drag racer, can travel over 600 feet in less than three seconds. To do this, it reaches speeds of more than 270 miles per hour! This kind of super performance is tough on tires. How long do you think one of these high-tech tires will last? To find out, start at the letter marked with a white dot. Move clockwise around the circle picking up every third letter. Write them on the lines below.

A tire on a top fuel racecar lasts about

T H _ _ _ _ _ _ _ _ _ _ _ _ _ !

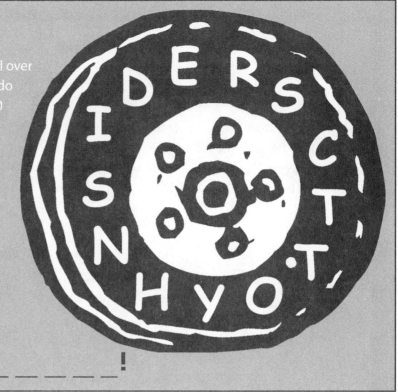

Quick Fix

This mechanic is yelling for help. He has only seconds to get everything for the racer's pit stop! See how quickly you can help him find the hidden word in each sentence. The things you are looking for are in the list, but be careful—there are extras!

1. "Jerry, find Jeff a new jacket and helmet!"
2. "Ricky, donuts and coffee, PRONTO!"
3. "Bob, rake the soil off the track!"
4. "This is no time for fun, Nelson!"
5. "J.R.! A 'G' size bulb, and hurry!"
6. "What a snafu! Eleven broken pins!"
7. "J.B., ol' T.S. here needs a battery, NOW!"

wrench	oil
nuts	bolts
fuel	jack
pliers	brake
funnel	rags
light	tires
filters	clamp

Racecar

At the pit stop, the pit crew races to change the tires and fill the car with fuel as quickly as possible. How fast can you figure out all these words that include the letters R-A-C-E or C-A-R?

__ __ __ R A C E = *a patio*

C A R __ __ __ = *a floor covering*

__ __ __ R A C E = *to hug*

C A R __ __ __ __ = *sticky, brown candy*

__ R A C E = *short prayer said before a meal*

__ __ __ C A R = *part of a train used to carry freight*

__ R A C E __ __ __ = *jewelry worn on the wrist*

C A R __ __ __ __ __ = *a fair that has games and rides*

__ R A C E __ = *copies lines through a piece of thin paper*

__ C A R __ = *a piece of cloth worn about the neck*

R A C E __ __ __ __ __ = *a place where cars race*

__ C A R __ __ __ __ __ = *straw person used to scare birds*

__ R A C E __ = *metal wires used to straighten teeth*

C A R __ __ __ __ __ __ = *thick paper used to make boxes*

Ready... Set... Search

How quickly can you find the one time PIT STOP is spelled correctly? Look sharp—the answer can be side to side, top to bottom, or even bottom to top!

EXTRA FUN: Can you find one PISTON?

```
P T T S T O P
I T O T O P I
T P S O S O T
S O P P T T S
T S I S O S O
T I S P I T P
O S T O P I T
P T O T I P O
I T N S T P P
P I T S O O P
```

Zzzzzzzz

Break the Nutz 'n' Boltz Code to find the silly answer to this riddle:

Why don't racecars use mufflers?

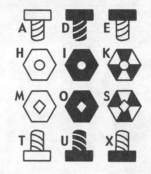

Ouch

Work the equation under each letter. Then put the letters on the correct dotted lines.

O
10+3

What kind of shot does a mechanic give a sick racecar?

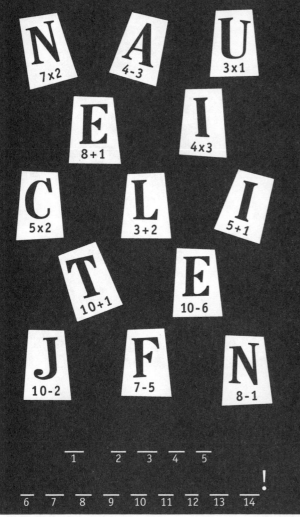

N
7×2

A
4−3

U
3×1

E
8+1

I
4×3

C
5×2

L
3+2

I
5+1

T
10+1

E
10−6

J
10−2

F
7−5

N
8−1

‾1 ‾2 ‾3 ‾4 ‾5

‾!

‾6 ‾7 ‾8 ‾9 ‾10 ‾11 ‾12 ‾13 ‾14

No, Really

The joke to the left will make you chuckle, but the answer isn't correct! To learn the truth about race-car engines, start in one of the four corners of the grid. Read the letters in a logical order, one after the other, as you spiral into the center.

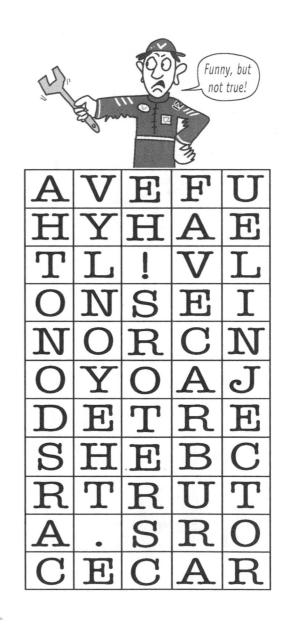

Funny, but not true!

A	V	E	F	U
H	Y	H	A	E
T	L	!	V	L
O	N	S	E	I
N	O	R	C	N
O	Y	O	A	J
D	E	T	R	E
S	H	E	B	C
R	T	R	U	T
A	.	S	R	O
C	E	C	A	R

Super Charged

Drag racers don't use gasoline. Their fuel is called "nitromethane." This fuel produces an awesome effect! What should you expect to see? Use an orange marker to color in the boxes with the letters D, R, and G. Read the remaining letters from top to bottom and left to right. Color these boxes yellow. Then color the rest of the picture!

Pit-ty Fast

During a race, a driver can make a pit stop to get tires, fuel, and repairs. The pit crew rushes to change all four tires, fill the fuel cell, adjust weight-carrying springs, and clean the grill and windshield. How fast can they do all that? To find out, cross out all boxes with a number 2, 4, or 7. Read the leftover boxes from left to right and top to bottom!

FOUR	THEY	74	43	CAN
DO	ALL	22	THAT	24
42	SEVEN	IN	TWO	AS
LITTLE	AS	34	15	72
47	28	OR	16	TWO
27	SECONDS	SEVEN	48	24

Do the Hustle

To encourage crews to go faster, sponsors hold pit crew competitions! See if you can make five words that all mean FAST. Start on the left, and use one letter in each column as you move from left to right. We left you a quick hint in each row! You can use each letter only once!

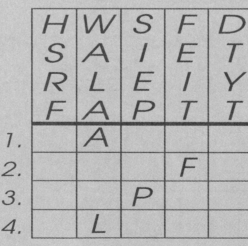

What 2 Fix?

This mechanic has a list of repairs—but which car needs what? The crew chief said to match each car to a picture on the list. Help R.P. pick the right job for each car!

Hint: One car gets two repairs!

BRAKES

OIL

AIR FILTER

STRUTS

GAS LINE

Racing Relay

What could be more fun than hosting a road race at home with all of your friends? Follow these directions for a zooming good time!

You will need:
2 bicycle helmets
2 different colored T-shirts
2 cardboard racing cars
1 race course

top flaps removed or tucked in

bottom flaps folded out and cut to make wheels

have around the house. Be creative. Give your car decals, headlights, numbers, racing stripes, and even sponsors!

MAKE A CARDBOARD RACING CAR

Find two cardboard boxes of the same size. They must be big enough for you to stand inside. Remove all the flaps so that you have only a cardboard rectangle.

Cut two handle holes on either side. You will use these to hold the car up while you are racing.

Decorate both cars with paints, markers, colored paper, or whatever you

MAKE A RACE COURSE

Set up a "track" in your yard. It can be as easy as making a start line, then racing around the outside of the house and returning to the start. You can make it more complicated by adding other obstacles to go around, such as chairs, trees, or rocks. In any case, all racers should clearly understand the track so they don't race off the course.

The Race

Divide your friends into even-numbered teams. If you have an odd number of people, one friend will have to race twice, or the extra person can be the race official who gives the start signal.

To start, one person on each team puts on the helmet and the T-shirt, then gets into the car. Racers lift the car off the ground using the handle holes. The racer must remain at the start line until given the signal. This could be as simple as you saying "Ready, Set, Go!", but you could also wave a flag to start the race. A napkin taped to a stick makes an easy flag.

On the signal, the cars race around the course. When they return to the start line, they must get out of the car, take off the helmet and T-shirt, and pass them all on to the next driver. Racer number two cannot leave the start line until he or she is fully dressed and in the car. The race continues until everyone has had a chance to drive the course. The first team to get all their drivers back to the start line wins.

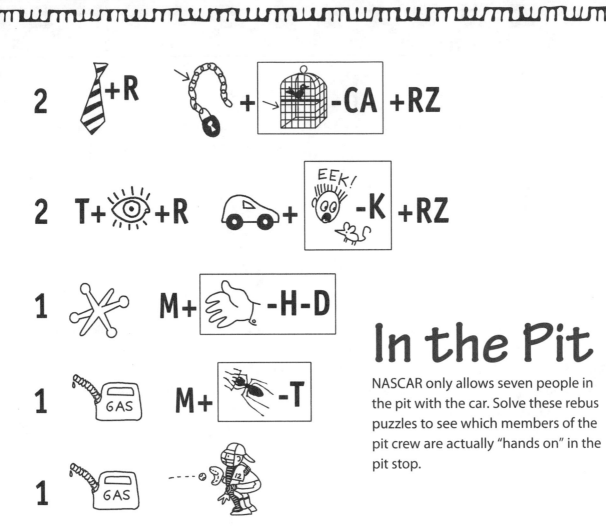

In the Pit

NASCAR only allows seven people in the pit with the car. Solve these rebus puzzles to see which members of the pit crew are actually "hands on" in the pit stop.

Every member of the pit crew is important, even the one who does his job from behind the wall that goes around the track! He uses a special long pole to reach out and into the car. Why? Break the First-to-Last Code to find out!

**EH IVESG
HET RIVERD
A RINKD!**

CHAPTER 3:
START YOUR ENGINES

Photo Finish

These four cars have just screeched across the finish line. They are so close, it's hard to tell who the winner is! Use the clues to figure out in what order these cars finished.

#6 finished ahead of #8 but not ahead of #24 and #4.

#24 did not cross the line just before #6.

FAST LAPS

How quickly can you make three different words by rearranging all the letters in the word LAPS? On your mark...get set...go!

_____

_____

_____

What a Gimmick

A gimmick rally is a race event with a puzzle to solve. It's kind of like auto racing mixed with a scavenger hunt, obstacle course, and card game! In this rally, racers must alternate left-right-left around traffic cones. The gimmick is that cars may only travel around the same type of cone as the one at their starting gate. Connect the beginning and end of each car's track to see who followed the pattern and is the winner!

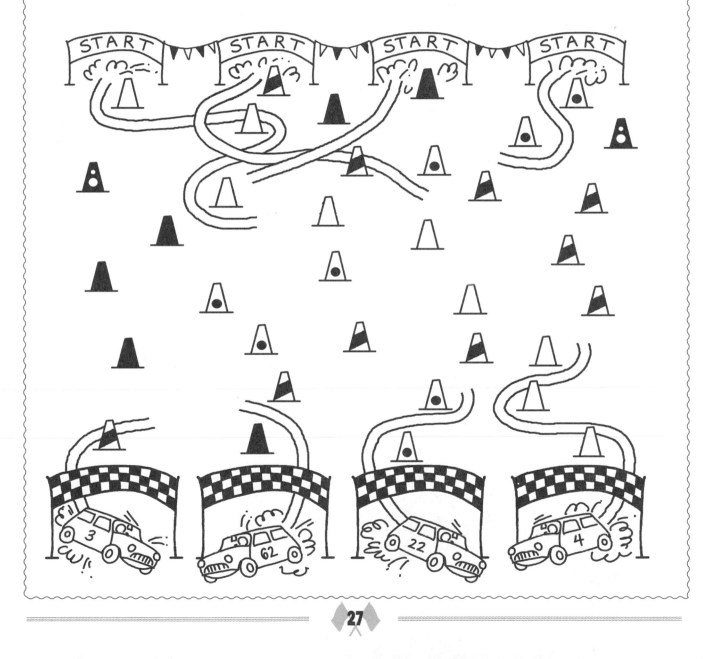

22   42

34   75

56

59   97

23

12   63

Who Is #1?

Fans can see how their favorite cars are doing by watching the lighted tower in the infield. This shows the constantly changing order of the cars. Take the car numbers listed above and put them in the tower from lowest to highest, starting at the top of the tower. The winner of this race was the car in the sixth spot. Which car was it?

1 _____
2 _____
3 _____
4 _____
5 _____
6 _____
7 _____
8 _____
9 _____
10

Keeping Pace

A pace car leads the racecars three times around the track before the race begins. This gives the drivers time to warm up their engines and tires and make absolutely sure that their cars are performing properly. How quickly can you figure out these ten words that rhyme with PACE?

To run after = _ _ _ _ _

A location = _ _ _ _ _

The front of the head = _ _ _ _

Area between things = _ _ _ _ _

Small bit left behind = _ _ _ _ _

Bottom of a mountain = _ _ _ _

Event for fast cars = _ _ _ _

Card worth most points = _ _ _

To hold steady = _ _ _ _ _

Prayer before dinner = _ _ _ _ _

I Spy

Here are some things you would expect to see at any racetrack! Find these three groups in the puzzle grid.

Which picture appears only once?

GROUP 1

GROUP 2

GROUP 3

Find a Track

NASCAR has racetracks all over the United States. Can you fit all the ones listed into the grid? We've left you some T-R-A-C-K-S to get you started!

EXTRA FUN: Add up the numbers in the tracks that don't have a state name. Match the sums with the two-letter state abbreviations to see where these tracks are located!

Atlanta   Daytona   Lowe's   Phoenix
Bristol   Dover   Kentucky   Talladega
California   Las Vegas   New Hampshire   Texas

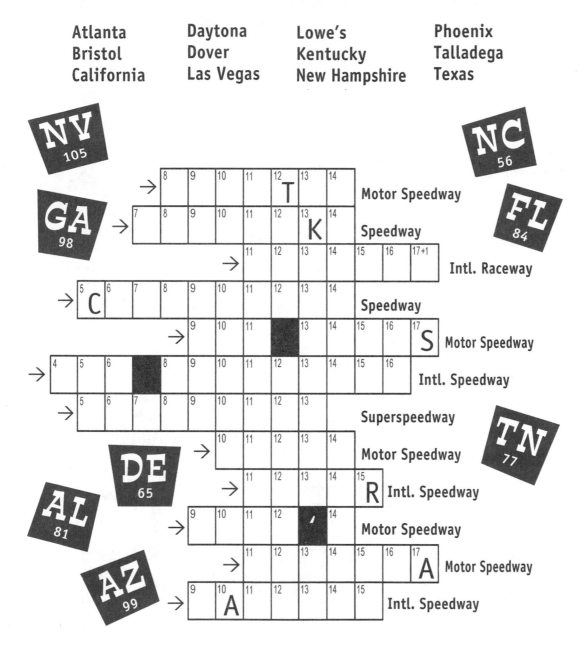

TRACK TYPES

Most races in the United States are held on three types of tracks:

short tracks
intermediates
superspeedways

All these tracks are basically oval shaped, with a short track being less than a mile around, and super-speedways being more than two miles. An intermediate is between one and two miles!

A very different type of track is called a "road course." To find out what that means, begin at the starting line on the letter marked with a dot. Pick up every other letter as you race counterclockwise around the track. You will need to make two laps to get all the letters and learn the answer!

The track letters, reading around: N K R A U M T S D R N E A V H I T R H D G E I S R R D U N O A C T D F A E O L R H A T N O O B S E N

THE COLOR OF VICTORY

At the racetrack you will see a variety of flags. Each has its own particular meaning. Unscramble the letters next to each flag to learn what color it should be. Then use crayons or markers to color in each flag! Hint: The meaning under each flag is a clue to that flag's color.

REGEN

start race

LOWYEL

caution

CLABK

penalty

DRE

stop

LUBE

passing

TIHEW

last lap

CREDCHEEK

end of race

Checkered Flag

The checkered flag is probably the most familiar of all racing flags. It shows that the race is over and there is a winner! To see which car has won each of these races, complete the checkered flags like this: each row, column, and corner-to-corner diagonal must add up to be the same number. This is the number of the winning car! The first flag has been done for you.

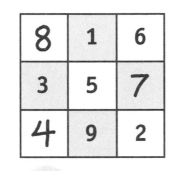

8	1	6
3	5	7
4	9	2

/15

	3	8
5	7	
6		4

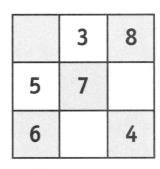

5	6	
	4	8
7		3

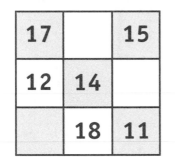

17		15
12	14	
	18	11

13	4	
6		12
8	14	

		1
3	6	9
5		2

GRAPH TRACKS

Have fun staging your own car races on the track provided—and on other tracks that you design yourself. All you need are two racecar drivers (yourself and a friend), colored pencils or markers, one standard dice, and graph paper (for other races).

Preliminaries

Each racer chooses a colored marker or pencil to represent his or her car then marks an X as a starting point in a square at the starting line.

The Race Begins

Racers choose who goes first. The first racer throws the dice to see how many squares he can move for his turn. Racers can move left, right, forward, or diagonally. They must move one square at a time to get to their new point, which they mark with an X. A straight line is then drawn in their color from their starting point to their new point. Each racer in turn throws the dice and decides how to move.

Rules of the Race

- No two racers can occupy the same spot at the same time. That would be a crash and would eliminate both of you!
- Cars can cross over each other's paths but cannot end up on the same square.
- If you can't move without crashing into someone, then you must stay in the same spot for that turn.

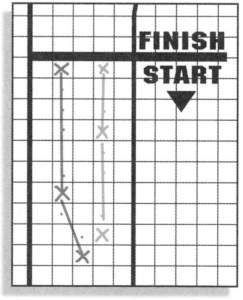

SAMPLE

Winning

The first racer to cross the finish line wins!

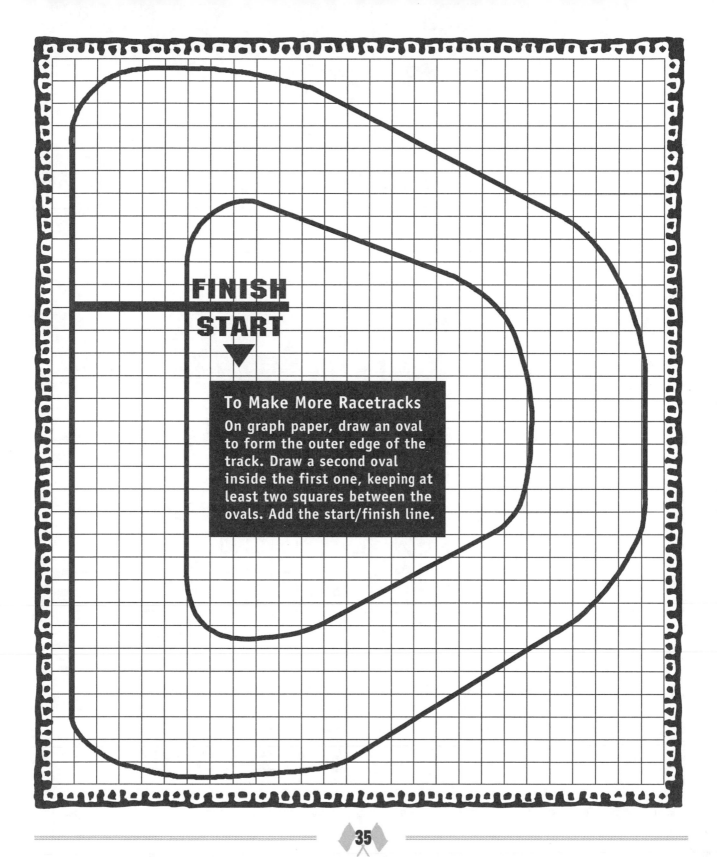

FINISH
START

To Make More Racetracks

On graph paper, draw an oval to form the outer edge of the track. Draw a second oval inside the first one, keeping at least two squares between the ovals. Add the start/finish line.

WHO WINS?

The finish line is an important part of any race, but it is most important to one special person. Who is that? Follow the directions to find out. Your answer will be three words.

FINISH | LINE

delete NI	delete LI
add R in middle	add O to beginning
change H to T	add one more word that means "from one side to the other"

Finish Line

In the 1992 Indy 500, Al Unser, Jr., crossed the finish line just fractions of a second before Scott Goodyear and was the winner! To see how close these two cars were, color in each box containing a horizontal "finish" line.

Al won by just

/			–	–	–	/	–	\	–	\			–	–	–
		/	–	/	–	/	–			–	\	/			\	–
\			–			–			–	–	–	–			/	–	–
		/	–	\	–	\			–			\	/	/	–
–	/	–	–	–	\	/	/	–	\	/	–	–	–

of a second!

36

Victory Plus

Along with the cash, the winner of each race gets something else. To find out what that is, use the clues to fill in the flags. The last letter of one word is the first letter of the next. When you have finished, write the letters in the white flags on the dotted lines. Hint: Fill the flags in order, even if it looks like you are spelling backward!

1. **Water from the eye**

2. **To do again**
3. **"I made a mistake!"**

4. **After fifth**
5. **Food for a horse**

Each winner also gets a

— — — — — — —

EXTRA FUN: CONNECT THE DOTS TO SEE THE PRIZE!

FAST TWENTY

Sponsorship is a big word that means big money for racecar teams. Team sponsors are companies that pay racing expenses. They give millions of dollars a year to have their name on the cars and on the drivers' uniforms. In return, millions of fans see this form of advertising at each race, and the sponsors make money because of it. How fast can you cash in on the twenty smaller words that are hiding in the word S-P-O-N-S-O-R-S-H-I-P?
Careful—you can use each letter only as many times as it appears in the word. For example, you can spell a word with two Os, but only one N.

SPONSORSHIP

1. _____   11. _____

2. _____   12. _____

3. _____   13. _____

4. _____   14. _____

5. _____   15. _____

6. _____   16. _____

7. _____   17. _____

8. _____   18. _____

9. _____   19. _____

10. _____ 20. _____

Decal Decision

Sponsors have created these coded sayings to use as decals on their race car. Can you figure out what each decal says, and which one is the most appropriate to use on the car? Write the best answer across the side of the car.

QTPIE	1DRFUL
10SNE1	42N8
4EVRL8	A4DABL
XLR8	NVR1

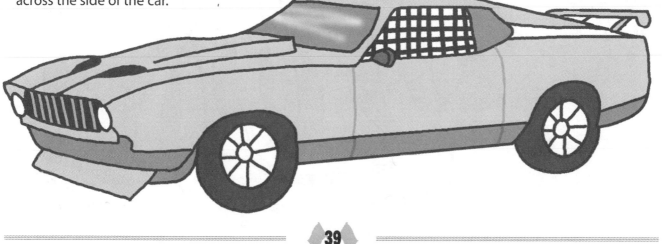

Get Me to the Race

Transporters are an important, and costly, part of every race team. These fifty-foot long giant rigs haul cars, tools, parts, and crew back and forth across the country to all the races. In addition to the cost of the transport equipment itself (easily $300,000 per rig), there are also the costs of food and gas along the way. This can be an additional $100,000 in expenses a year!

Help this transporter make its way from Race 1 to Race 2. You can travel over and under other roads, but this big rig can't make sharp turns. Smooth curves only!

Tons of Tires

Racecars wear out tires very rapidly. Cars can easily use up to twenty tires in one race! At about $1,600 per set, how much do you think a NASCAR team spends on tires every season?
To find out, look at the pairs of tires below. Some look like they are linked through each other. Others look like two tires that overlap but are not linked. Color in the letters on the tire pairs that are linked. Read the white letters (left to right, top to bottom) that remain in the unlinked tires.

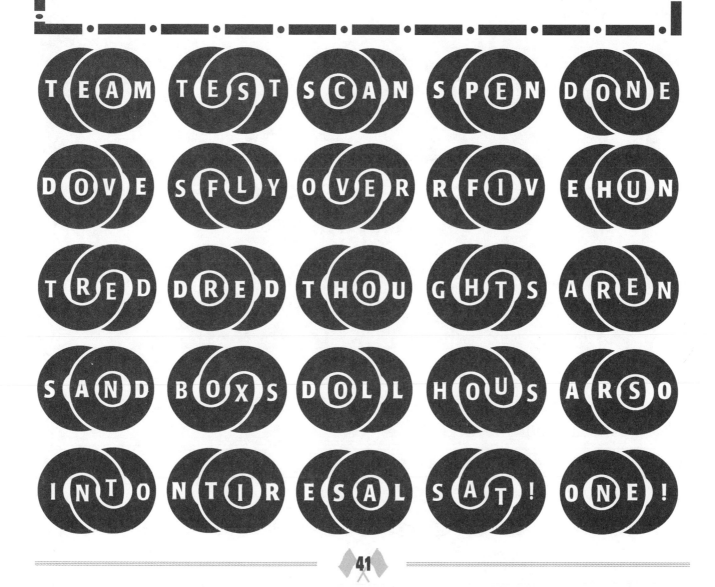

CRAZY MONEY

Formula One racecars are super fast, high tech, and wickedly expensive. Each car has over 5,000 parts, each engineered to perfection. For example, it can cost $120,000 to build just one very familiar car part for a Formula One racer! To find out which part can cost this much, break the Number Substitution Code (1=A, 2=B, 3=C, etc.)

12•5•5•8•23

7•14•9•18•5•5•20•19

Oops, forgot to mention that the answe is totally backwards!

Hink Pinks

Drivers, sponsors, and owners may enjoy the sport of auto racing just as much as the fans, but they are always looking at the profit, too! See if you can solve all of these silly "hink pinks" that have to do with money. Wait a minute—what's a hink pink? A pair of one-syllable words that rhyme!

A money run = **C** _ _ _   **D** _ _ _

One dollar good fortune = **B** _ _ _   **L** _ _ _

A wealthy spell caster = **R** _ _ _   **W** _ _ _ _

Smart thing you won = **W** _ _ _   **P** _ _ _ _

Sweet cash from bees = **H** _ _ _ _   **M** _ _ _ _

A money toss = **D** _ _ _ _ _   **T** _ _ _ _

Many Sponsors

Big-league racing teams can easily spend $300,000 per race. You can see why they need to have a lot of sponsors! These drivers are wearing the logos of companies that sponsor their team. Which two logos do not appear on the suits and head-gear of both drivers?

Thank You, Jimmie!

How much money drivers make each year is not really known. However, how much money they earn for their team by winning races every season is certainly known. Cross out all the numbers 2, 3, 5, 6, and 7 in this grid. Drop the remaining numbers into the boxes at the bottom to see the total winnings for Jimmie Johnson, the 2006 Nextel Cup winner.

2	3	5	9	7	2	5
8	5	6	3	6	5	6
6	9	7	2	7	3	3
2	7	3	5	1	6	7
3	2	5	6	7	4	2
5	3	6	7	3	7	0
7	6	0	2	5	2	6

$ | | | | | | | |

EXTRA FUN: Jimmie Johnson's car, #48, is owned by another very successful NASCAR driver. In fact, this man won the Daytona 500 six times! Crack the 1=A Code to find his name. Hint: His car is #24.

10 - 5 - 6 - 6
7 - 15 - 18 - 4 - 15 - 14

SKY'S THE LIMIT

While racecars are being shuttled cross-country in giant transporters, racing teams—not only the drivers, but mechanics, pit crews, engineers, and support staff—need to get to the track, too. If an owner has more than one team at a race, that's a huge number of people to move, and quickly! How do the teams keep up with the crazy race schedules? Break the Backward Last-to-First Code to find out.

YOW! I GOTTA BE THERE FRIDAY?!

SCHEDULE

anyM eamst wno nda

perateo everals malls

lanesp. neO wnero,

iredt fo eepingk rackt

fo ish 61 Lanesp ache

acer eekendw, inallyt

oughtb hreet 277 etsj!

RACE DAY, PAYDAY

Believe it or not, the winner of a race doesn't always take home the most money that day. A driver that finishes behind the winner might earn one or more special awards that would make his or her total earnings higher! Use the information provided to calculate the winnings of each driver.

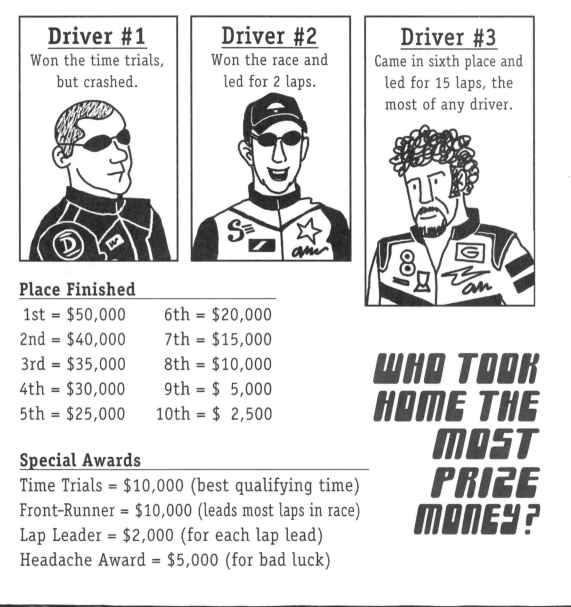

Driver #1
Won the time trials, but crashed.

Driver #2
Won the race and led for 2 laps.

Driver #3
Came in sixth place and led for 15 laps, the most of any driver.

Place Finished

1st = $50,000	6th = $20,000
2nd = $40,000	7th = $15,000
3rd = $35,000	8th = $10,000
4th = $30,000	9th = $ 5,000
5th = $25,000	10th = $ 2,500

Special Awards

Time Trials = $10,000 (best qualifying time)

Front-Runner = $10,000 (leads most laps in race)

Lap Leader = $2,000 (for each lap lead)

Headache Award = $5,000 (for bad luck)

WHO TOOK HOME THE MOST PRIZE MONEY?

$how Me the Money

A racecar driver earns money in several different ways. To learn what they are, make a three-letter word on each line by placing a letter in the empty middle box. Choose from the letters to the right of the grid. When you have used all the letters, read down the shaded columns to learn the main sources of income for drivers. We left you some $$$$ to get started! Hint: $=S

answer

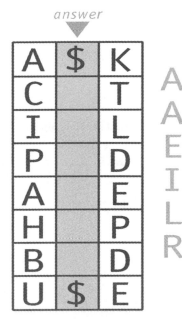

Letters: A A E I L R

answer

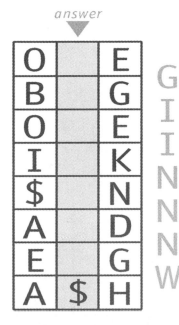

Letters: G I I N N N W

answer

P		N
I		N
A		D
M		M
E		A
A	$	K
$		A
E		U
B		E
A		T
I		$
U	$	E

Letters: D E E E M N N O R T

Big Bucks

BMUOCRETHKAN
CBU5CSKOSBUCK
BMUIULCLCIOKN
SBAUYBECAKRUS

Drivers at the start of their racing careers barely make enough to cover expenses. But top-level Formula One drivers like Michael Schumacher can earn a lot! How much does he make in a year? To find out, fill in the letters B-U-C-K-S. Read the remaining letters from left to right and top to bottom.

Top Dollar

Which racing series allows their drivers to make the most money? To find out, start by fitting all the words into the grid. We left some D-O-L-L-A-R-S and C-E-N-T-S to help you out! When you're finished, take the shaded letters from left to right and top to bottom and place them in order on the dotted lines.

4 letters
cars
team
open
axle

5 letters
rules   world
gears   alarm
speed   dents
event

6 letters
racing

7 letters
promote
circuit
factory
engines

answer ▶ _ _ _ _ _ _ _ _ _ _ _

CHAPTER 5:
FAN-TASTIC FUN

SAD FAN, GLAD FAN

Race fans can be happy or sad depending on what is happening to their favorite driver during a race. Help this crowd's mood improve by making a path that alternates sad fans with glad fans. You can move up and down, or side to side, but not diagonally. If you get to a crazy fan, go another way!

START

END

Listen Up

Smart racing fans wear some very important gear to protect them-selves from the noise at the racetrack. To find out what that is, fol-low the directions to fill in the blocks on the signs these fans are holding.

Fill in...

...all the blocks on the left side of every sign except 8.

...all the blocks on the right side of signs 2 and 6.

...all the blocks across the top of signs 1, 2, 3, 4, 7, and 8.

...all the blocks across the bottom of signs 1, 5, 6, 7, and 8.

...just the center block of signs 1, 2, 3, 4, and 8.

...the blocks with a dot in the middle.

RACING FAST FACT

A decibel, or dB, is a mea-sure of loudness.

a whisper = 20 dB
vacuum cleaner = 80 dB
jackhammer = 100 dB
one stock car running at
full speed = 130 dB

ALL BUBBA'D UP

Except for their size, these father and son race fans look the same.
Can you find the ten ways in which their outfits and souvenirs are different?

Fan Fun

Each sentence needs one letter to complete all the words. Have fun figuring out the silly things these race fans are doing!

__rantic __amilies __lap __estive __lags.

__razy __ouples __arry __ardboard __utouts.

__ild __omen __ave __acky __ooden __ands.

__ischievous __en __ake __onkey __oves.

__heering __hildren __ast __olorful __onfetti.

- -

Fans in the Stands

Can you find your way from START to END through these funny fans?

WHAT A FAN

You can find race F-A-Ns just about anywhere—
even in other words! See how many of these you
know. Hint: Use the letters in dark boxes to fill in
the blanks. Each letter or letter pair is used only
once! Careful—there's one extra letter pair.

A long, pointed tooth = **FAN** __

Amazing! = **FAN** __ __ __ __ __ __

An imaginative story = **FAN** __ __ __ _

Very decorated = **FAN** __ __

Rear end nickname = **FAN** __ __

Baby = __ __ **FAN** __

Cool, Baby!

There is a silly riddle and its silly answer hidden in the border of this
page. You must figure which word is first, and in which direction to read
around the page.

the fans!

They

TAS

CY

cool?

How

AT

SY

do

stay

Made in the Shade

These race fans are camping on the infield in an RV (recreational vehicle). Can you find which shadow pattern is a perfect match for their vehicle?

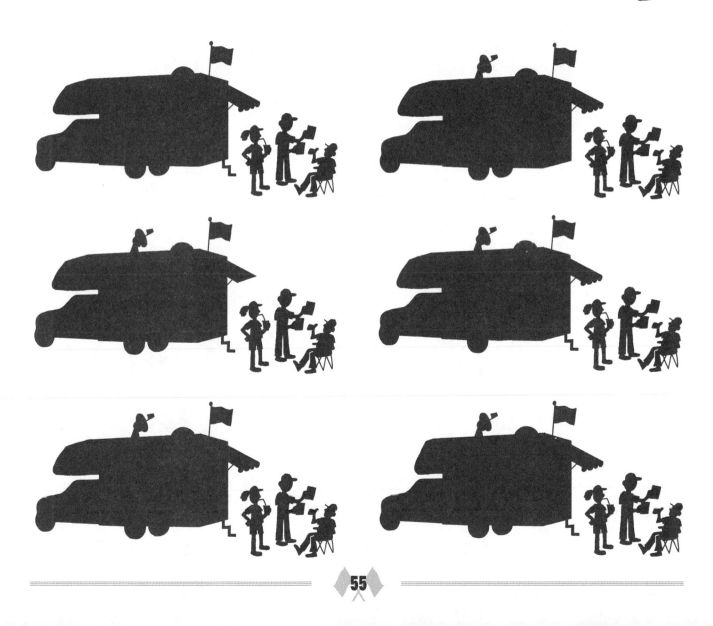

Second to One

Race fans used to be found mostly in the southern United States where the sport was born. Now, with tracks in almost every state and huge media coverage, people everywhere watch stock car races. In fact, there is only one sport in this country with more fans! Follow the directions to find out which sport that is.

— **Each clue suggests a five-letter word ending with E.**

— **Write each word into the puzzle. Place the first letter in the outer ring and spell towards the middle.**

— **When you are done, read the letters in the outer ring. Start with number 1, and read counterclockwise.**

1. *Wooden barrier around a yard*

2. *A small fruit pressed for oil*

3. *Overly fat*

4. *Number that follows two*

5. *Holy book*

6. *A fruit used for pies*

7. *The opposite of small*

8. *To exit*

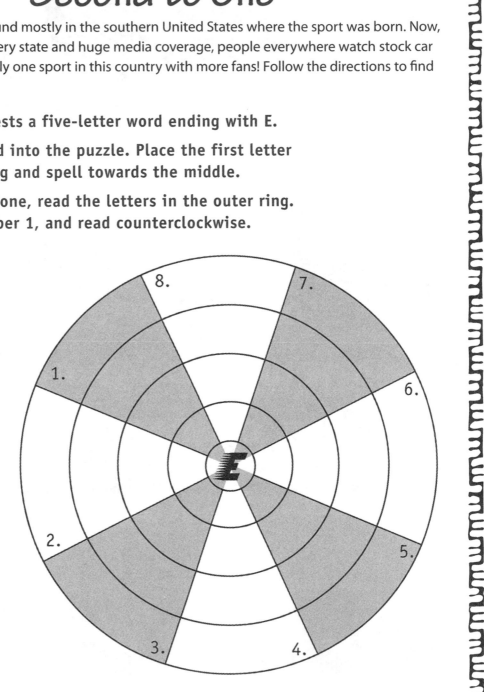

Sign This, Please?

This fan has been collecting NASCAR drivers' autographs for years. Unfortunately, some of the signatures have gotten worn away! Can you figure out which autograph belongs to which driver?

Possible Drivers:

Kyle Busch

Dale Earnhardt

Jeff Gordon

Kevin Harvick

Jimmie Johnson

Matt Kenseth

Bobby Labonte

Richard Petty

Tony Stewart

Rusty Wallace

Super Souvenirs

NASCAR figures about 75 million fans regularly travel to the tracks, and a lot of them buy souvenirs before they leave. Add this to fans who buy from specialty shops, catalogs, and online, and you are talking a huge amount of retail sales! How much are fans spending? To find out, find all the items from the word list hidden in the letter grid. Then read the remaining letters from left to right and top to bottom.

BOOK
CALENDAR
CLOCK
DECAL
DIE CAST CAR
DOLL
FLAG
HAT
HELMET
JACKET
KEYCHAIN
MAGNET
MUG
PAJAMAS
PHOTOGRAPH
POSTER
SHEETS
SOCKS
SUNGLASSES
SWEATSHIRT
T SHIRT
TENT
TOWEL
TRADING CARD
VISOR
WATCH

Helpful hint: Try highlighting each word as you find it with a single line from a colored marker. It's easier than circling with a pencil!

```
L S A M A J A P R W A T C H D
E E T C G A L F D E C A L A O
W H I L S W E A T S H I R T L
O A L O S A L E E S O E S S L
T T F C L I K C E N T S O H E
D N A K S C O C A S R M C I E
C R H C A H O A O N D I K R S
A T E J E I B P S N O W S T O
L E L V E R T N I A H C Y E K
E N M U G W O B I V I S O R L
N T E L I D I E C A S T C A R
D O T R A D I N G C A R D N D
A S H E E T S O L M A G N E T
R L A R S S E S S A L G N U S
A Y P H O T O G R A P H E A R
```

TRAFFIC JAM

Too many fans are trying to get to the racetrack at the same time. Can you help the van full of fans find the "back way" and beat the traffic to the parking lot?

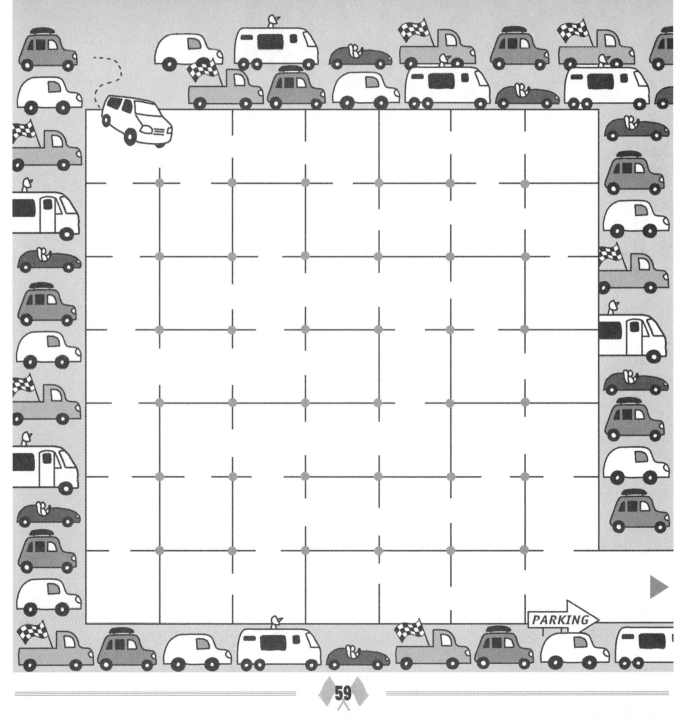

```
Z2W693X4O2
O42602F2AZY
N2S2FYZR2O
ZX2W4M2612
82OZ2C2ZOW
Z2U2YN42XX
T2R2I2E62WS
```

Wow!

The International Automobile Federation wanted to know what fans thought about Formula One racing. Officials were amazed by the huge number of fans from around the world who took the online survey. In fact, the Web site crashed because there were so many people trying to take the survey! How many is that? To find out, fill in the numbers 2, 4, and 6 and the letters W, X, Y, and Z. Read the remaining numbers and letters from left to right and top to bottom.

Feel Like a Fan

Break the Alphabet Shift Code (A=B, B=C, C=D, etc.) to find a word that describes something that all race fans have!

CHAPTER 6:
CRASH!

Crash Cross

Many forceful words are used when describing a racecar crash! Each clue below will suggest a word from the word list. Use these words to fill in the crossword grid. All the words will fit correctly in only one way. We left you some FLAMES and DEBRIS to get you started.

ACROSS
4. A crash
5. To slip sideways
7. To turn over once
9. To ruin completely
10. Harm done to a person
12. Lights shooting from burning gasoline
13. To come apart

DOWN
1. To spring back up
2. To hit with force
3. To turn over and over
5. To turn around quickly
6. Bits and pieces left after a crash
7. To move through the air
8. A ruined car
11. Rise quickly up into the air

BOUNCE
BREAK
COLLISION
DEBRIS
DESTROY
FLAMES
FLIP
FLY
INJURY
JUMP
ROLL
SLAM
SLIDE
SPIN
WRECK

CRAZY CRASH

Two drivers are e-mailing each other about a crash earlier in the day. Crack the keyboard code to see what they are saying!

Driver #1: **Y92   E8E   697   JQHQT3   59**

D4QWY 8H 5Y3 OQW5 4QD3P

Driver #2: E8E   697   W33   5YQ5   G8T

D74F3 9H 5Y3 RQ4 W8E3

9R 5Y3 54QDIP

Driver #1: **63WP**

Driver #2: 2300K 8 E8EH&5?

Double Trouble

In 2000, there were two fatal wrecks at the New Hampshire International Speedway. Adam Petty and Kenny Irwin died when their car throttles stuck and they crashed full speed into the wall. After these tragedies, NASCAR made teams add a new safety feature to cars. To find out what it was, figure out which letters are described by each fraction. Print the letters, in order, from left to right in the boxes below.

1. First ½ of KICK
2. Last ½ of WALL
3. First ⅖ of SWEAT
4. Middle ¾ of HITS
5.. Last ½ OUCH

Sounds Bad

The safety feature described above has a name that sounds bad. But this device doesn't hurt a driver, it saves him or her! How does it work? Break the Last-to-First Code to find out.

heT illk witchs urnst ffo a ar'sc lectricale owerp, ro "illsk" het nginee, ot lows het arc ownd fi het hrottlet etsg tucks.

OH SO HOT

All clothing that racecar drivers wear is fire retardant—even their underwear! But they pay extra attention to make sure that one part of their body is well protected from the heat.

To find out which body part that is—and why—figure out where to put the letters in each column of this puzzle. The letters all fit in the boxes under their own columns, but not always in the same order!

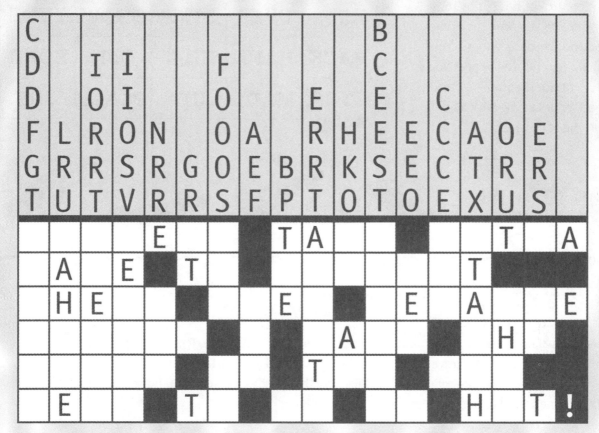

C D F G T	L R U	I O R R T	I I O S V	N R R	F O O G R	F O O S	A E F	B P	E R R T	H K O	B C E E S T	E E O	C C E	A T X	O R U	E R S
			E				T	A							T		A
A		E		T										T		
H	E					E				E		A			E
								A				H		
							T						
E			T							H		T	!

Why are drivers so worried about the heat? Color in each box with a dot in the center to find out how hot it gets inside the cockpit of a stock car on a summer day.

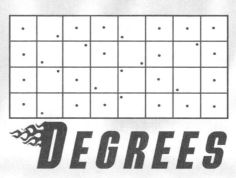

DEGREES

Rollover

Regain control of this car by moving one space at a time making compound words as you go. You can move up and down, and side to side, but not diagonally. If you succeed, your car will shortly be back in the road race!

START

ROLL	OVER	SIDE	SHOW	TUNE
BACK	HAND	HILL	OFF	ROAD
STEP	MADE	UP	SCALE	WAY

END

Draft Dodger

Drivers follow close behind other cars in a race to reduce air resistance. This technique is called "drafting," and it helps cars travel faster than if they traveled far apart on the track. But it only takes a tiny mistake to make many cars crash! Using the clues below, can you figure out which of the six cars managed to avoid a pileup?

Car #2 fishtails and bumps Car #1.

Car #1 hits Car #4 and they both hit the wall.

Car #1 bounces off the wall and hits Car #5.

Car #5 spins out and takes out Car #6 and Car #3.

Slow Down!

Daytona and Talladega are two "fast" tracks that have had many crashes. To increase driver safety, NASCAR makes all cars use a safety feature in their carburetors when driving on these tracks. These flat metal pieces with holes reduce the airflow to the engine and slow the cars down.

To see the name of this safety feature, solve the puzzle below. Each clue suggests a word. Write the word on the dotted lines and carefully copy each letter into the numbered grid.

1D	2B	3B	4D	5C	6A	7C	8C	9D	10A
	11A	12B	13C	14A	15C	16B			

A. To stumble

$\overline{14}$ $\overline{10}$ $\overline{6}$ $\overline{11}$

B. Opposite of more

$\overline{12}$ $\overline{2}$ $\overline{16}$ $\overline{3}$

C. Copy through thin paper

$\overline{8}$ $\overline{5}$ $\overline{13}$ $\overline{7}$ $\overline{15}$

D. To decay

$\overline{1}$ $\overline{9}$ $\overline{4}$

Bits and Pieces

Crash! Which of these four racecars do you get when you put the pieces at the top of this puzzle back together again?

CRASH COMMENTS

This pit crew is shaking their heads as they watch a crash caused by a driver's error. What are they muttering? To find out, write all the letters from the scattered pieces into their proper spaces in the grids. Hint: Match the pattern of the black boxes.

Pass in the Grass

One of the most famous saves in NASCAR history was at the Winston 500 in 1987. With ten laps to go, Bill Elliott bumped Dale Earnhardt, Sr.'s car onto the grassy infield. Everyone thought he would spin out and crash, but Dale kept control, drove through the grass, and got back onto the track. He not only saved his car from a wreck, but he won the race!

Help Dale's car (#3) through the infield and back onto the track.

Watch Out!

During a race, cars often drive over chunks of rubber tires, scraps of metal and plastic from crashes, and other bits of junk that fall on the track. This small stuff can cause big trouble by making a driver lose control of the car! Strangely, this dangerous track trash has a kind of cute nickname! Fill in all the shapes with the letters J-U-N-K to see what it is.

R+1= ____   Y+2= ____   H−2= ____   F−1 = ____   S−1 = ____

O+5= ____   R−4 = ____   J+5= ____   Q−3 = ____   A+4= ____

G−2 = ____   E−1 = ____   Z+1 = ____   B+3= ____   F−2 = ____

C+2 = ____   I+4 = ____   P+2 = ____   T+1 = ____

K+1= ____   J−3 = ____   Z+3 = ____

                                                     V+3= ____   U−1 = ____

Getting Safer

Since 2002, an ongoing project at racetracks is to provide SAFER barriers. These barriers are designed to lessen the impact for the driver in the event that they are hit. Solve the letter equations to see what the S-A-F-E-R letters stand for.

G+2 = ____

N+1= ____

S−5 = ____

70

Crunch!

Over time, safety devices have been created to help make racing a safer sport. Crashes still happen, however! In the puzzle below, some words have crashed into and become scrambled up with seven safety devices. Cross out the letters C-R-A-S-H, B-A-N-G, B-O-O-M, or S-Q-U-I-S-H that are hidden in each word. Read the remaining letters from left to right.

1. **WCIRNDOAWNSEHT**

2. **RSOQOFUFISLAPH**

3. **BFUOELOCELML**

4. **KIBLLSAWINTCGH**

5. **FIBREAPRONOFSGUK**

Totally Stuck

Ryan Newman crashed at the Daytona 500 in 2003. He destroyed his car but was not badly hurt. However, something unexpected got wedged in the driver's seat, keeping Ryan pinned in the wreckage! Do all three puzzles to see what it was.

Hint:
1=A
2=B
3=C

Hint: Dot 2 Dot

Hint: Vowel Switch

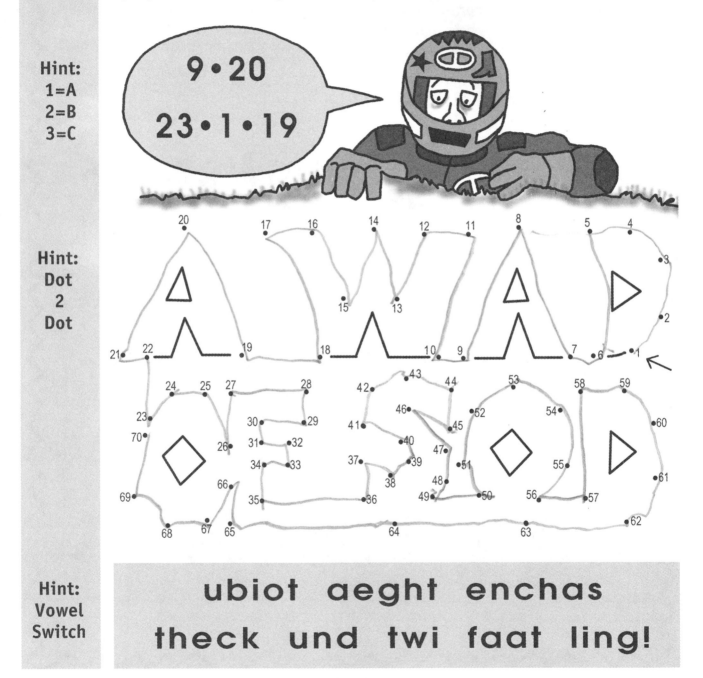

9•20
23•1•19

ubiot aeght enchas
theck und twi faat ling!

CHAPTER 7:
DO-IT-YOURSELF RACING

Cookie Cars

Ricky Racer decided to bake some sugar cookies for his pit crew. All of the cookies on the cooling rack came from one of these rolled-out batches of dough. Can you figure out which one?

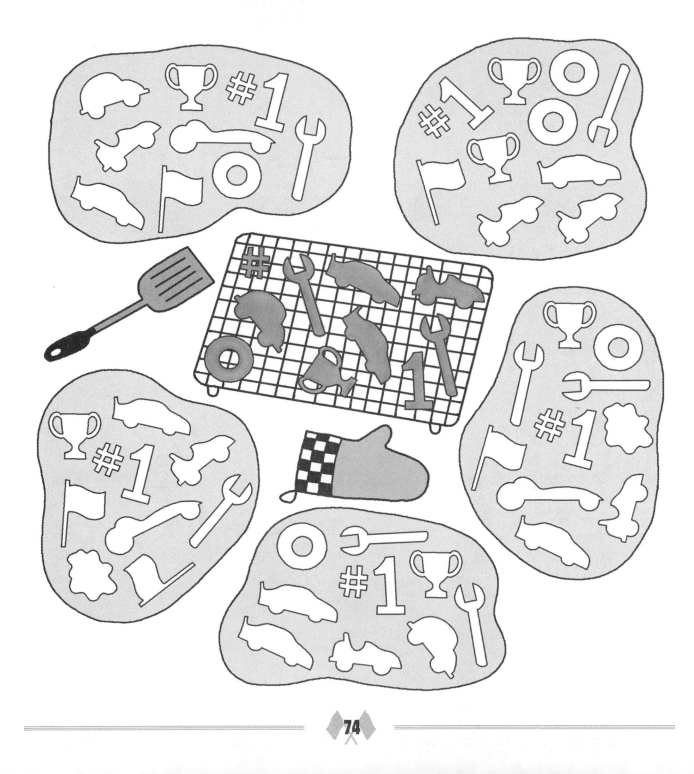

Bake Your Own Cookie Cars

You will need a tube of premade sugar cookie dough, ¾ cup white flour, a rolling pin, car-shaped cookie cutters, just the yolks of several eggs, liquid food coloring, a soft paint brush, assorted tiny candies (optional), and the help of an adult.

Take the dough out of the tube and gently knead in the flour. Roll and cut using the car-shaped cookie cutters.

Before baking is the time to give each car a fancy paint job! Mix an egg yolk with 1 tsp. of water. Mix drops of food coloring into the egg mixture until you get the color you want (not too dark). Use a craft brush with soft bristles to paint each car. When the base coat has dried you can go back with a darker color to add numbers or decals. Add additional details with small candies such as red hots, jimmies, candy confetti, or mini chocolate chips.

Have an adult help you to bake the cookies in a preheated 350°F oven for 8–10 minutes. Caution—cookies bake faster if you are using dark-colored cookie sheets! Cool finished cookies on wire racks.

JUST JOKING

It is fun to collect jokes about racing to tell your friends! Find all the words in the grid with the same number as each car. Rearrange the words to get the joke's answer.

2	hot	3	500!	1	What
2	They	1	a	3	Apple-less
4	driver!	3	The	4	screw
3	Indian	2	both	5	a
5	fast	5	pull	2	rods!
1	drag!	4	A	5	to
5	one!	5	Trying	2	are

Extra Fun: Use markers to color each car!

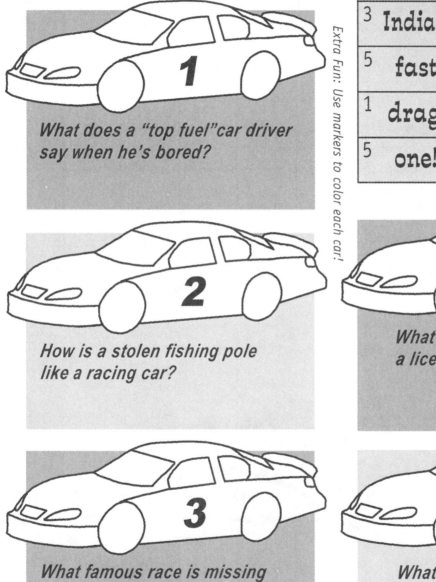

What does a "top fuel"car driver say when he's bored?

How is a stolen fishing pole like a racing car?

What famous race is missing some important fruit?

What driver doesn't have a license?

What was the sneaky tow truck doing at the race?

LOTS OF SLOTS

Slot cars are tiny, electric-powered cars. A pin on the bottom of the car fits into one of several slots, or grooves, in a plastic track. Several people race against each other, using hand-held controllers to steer. Slot-car racing is really fast and really fun!

Use letters from the track to finish the words with L-O-T. Then see which car has the most vowels in its slot. That car wins the race!

S

TERY

H

OCE

C

PI

1

H

___**LOT** = a lump of blood

___ ___**LOT** = person who flies a plane

___**LOT**___ = slow, tree-hanging animal

LOT___ ___ ___ = hand cream

___**LOT** = main story

___ ___ ___**LOT** = voting form

LOT___ ___ ___ ___ = a contest with numbered tickets

2

C

___ ___ ___**LOT** = small spotted wildcat

___**LOT**___ = fabric

___**LOT** = spot or stain

B

P

BAL

ION

Super Soap Boxes

Kids can't drive stock cars until they're adults, but they can build and get behind the wheel of a soap box car! These small cars are gravity powered and the races, or derbies, are run on hills. The 2006 World Championship in Akron, Ohio, hosted almost 500 racers and their families from over 40 different states!

To see how this soap box derby car was built, write the correct part number for each piece on the lines provided. We've given you a small picture of the completed car to guide you. Caution: Some of the pieces may be upside down!

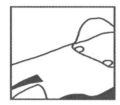

Part # _____

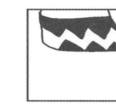

Part # _____

Part # _____

Part # _____

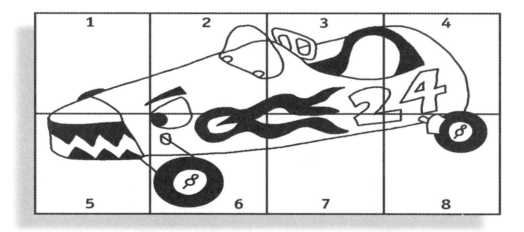

Part # _____

Part # _____

Part # _____

Part # _____

Red Light, Green Light

This classic game is easy to play and you don't have to be fast to win. You do, however, need to be able to start and stop quickly—and hold still when you stop! The game works best with at least four people.

WHAT YOU WILL NEED:

- A driveway and a piece of chalk, or a large activity room like the school gym.

BEFORE YOU START:

1. Draw a start and a finish line with the chalk, or decide which lines on the gym floor you will use. They should be far enough apart for a good race, but not so far that you can't hear the Caller.
2. Choose a "Caller." This player stands on the finish line with his back to the racers.
3. All the other players line up on the starting line.

TO PLAY:

1. When the Caller yells, "Green Light," everyone moves forward.
2. When the Caller yells, "Red Light," everyone must stop and stand completely still. The Caller whips around and tries to catch racers who are moving. If he catches anyone, that person goes back to the start line.
3. The game continues until someone reaches the finish line and tags the Caller. That racer becomes the Caller for the next game!

EXTRA FUN: Break the RLGL code to see which kid—1, 2, or 3—becomes the next caller!

RLGL Decoder
RL = red light
GL = green light
M = moved
Numbers = how many blocks towards the finish line.

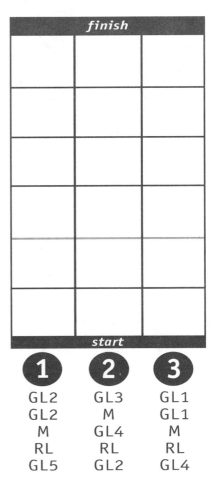

finish		
start		

1	**2**	**3**
GL2	GL3	GL1
GL2	M	GL1
M	GL4	M
RL	RL	RL
GL5	GL2	GL4

Double Trouble

Two friends are trying to guide their radio-controlled cars through this obstacle course. Can you help them each find a path from START to FINISH? Here's the tricky part—the paths can't cross each other!

START

FINISH

Zoom Zoom Zoom

Are you in the mood for a wild and crazy racing card game? All you need is a standard deck of cards and at least one friend. The object of the game is to collect all the cards as quickly as possible!

BEFORE YOU PLAY:

- Remove the jokers, kings, queens, and aces from the deck. Use just the numbers 2–10 (racecars) and the jacks (racecar drivers).
- The jacks (racecar drivers) are wild cards. They can be any number!
- Shuffle the cards and deal them equally among the players. If there are any extra cards, put them aside. Players should hold their cards face down.

TO PLAY:

1. Players chant together, "ZOOM, ZOOM, ZOOM!"
2. On the third ZOOM, each player flips over his top card into the center of the table.
3. If two of the same numbers are showing, players try to slap their hand down on top of the cards before anyone else does.
4. The player who is quickest wins the cards and adds them to the bottom of his own card pile.
5. If no pair is showing, repeat the ZOOM chant and flip another card.

ADDED FUN:

Use a clock or stopwatch to see how long it takes to win a game. Keep track of five games on a piece of paper. Out of the five games, who won most quickly? This player is the Super Zoomer!

Build and Eat Car Game

This is a fun game for hungry racecar fans. You win if you are the first player to build your own racecar. The bonus? All players get to eat their cars when the game is over!

For each player you will need:

1 paper plate or paper towel

1 small oblong snack cake

Several thin pretzel sticks

4 round hard candies with holes in the center

1 small lollipop (candy part should be round like a ball, not flat like a quarter)

Pair of dice (you will use just one of the pair, or one "die")

The numbers on the die stand for car parts:

1 = car body (snack cake)

2 = wheel axles (pretzel sticks)

3 = front wheels (hard candies with hole)

4 = back wheels (hard candies with hole)

5 = driver's seat (a small bite out of snack cake)

6 = lollipop (driver)

BEFORE YOU BEGIN:

1. Read the directions and building tips.
2. Unwrap the food items and place them in the center of the table on a plate or tray.
3. Each player gets a paper plate or towel on which to build a car.
4. All players roll the die. The person who gets the highest number goes first, then the other players take turns in a clockwise direction.

TO PLAY:

The racecars must be built in order—first the car body, then the axles, next the wheels, the seat, and, finally, the driver. Play continues until someone has their whole car built and rolls a 6 to add their driver.

1. Each player MUST roll a 1 to begin building the car.
2. If the first player doesn't roll a 1, it is the next player's turn.
3. If the first player does roll a 1, they take a car body (snack cake) and roll again to try for a 2, one of the axles (pretzel stick).
4. Each time a player adds a piece to their car, they get to roll again. If they roll a number they can't use, it is the next player's turn.
5. After a winner has been declared, all players should finish building their cars—and then everyone eats them!

BUILDING TIPS:

- **Wheel axles:** Slide the pretzel sticks through the snack cake about ½ inch up from the bottom to allow room for the wheels. If your pretzel sticks are too long and stick out too far on either side of the car, nibble or break them down to size.

- **Wheels:** If the hole in the center of your candy is not big enough to go over the pretzel stick easily, nibble or break the end of the pretzel stick to make it thinner. You could also use something skinnier for the axles (for example, raw spaghetti).

- **Driver's seat:** Remember, you must have all your wheels on the car and roll a 5 before you can make the driver's seat! To do this, take a small bite out of the top of your car closer to one end than the other. This bite will form a dent in which the driver will sit.

- **Driver:** The stick on your lollipop is probably too long. Break it so that there is only a short piece to hold it in your snack cake. If you have a choice of lollipops, look for one that is full and round like a ball, not flat and round like a quarter. Some lollipops even look like they are wearing helmets!

Race Bingo

This is a great game for a long car ride. All you need is the bingo board and a pencil! Hint: Be sure to use a pencil so you can erase your marks and play again.

1. Look for the items pictured.
2. When you spot one, draw a light X over that object.
3. To get BINGO you need a straight line of Xs across the board in any direction, including diagonally.

How fast did you get BINGO the first time? Play again later in the trip. Did you get BINGO more quickly?

EXTRA FUN: Traveling with a friend? If you each choose a different mark (like an X and an O) you can share the game board!

the word **START**

dark sports car

23 large dark numbers

helmet

gas pump

American flag

stack of tires

sunscreen

42 large white numbers

dark sunglasses

the word **FINISH**

bleachers

cap with a logo

traffic cone

white sports car

checkered pattern

CHAPTER 8:
BREAKING RECORDS

FAST AS YOU CAN

Most racecar records have to do with how fast cars can go. How quickly can you place the letter sets in their proper places to make all these G-O words? Hint: The definitions will suggest which letters you will use to complete each word.

Not silver = <u>G</u> <u>O</u> __ __

Turkey noise = <u>G</u> <u>O</u> __ __ __ __

Large ape = <u>G</u> <u>O</u> __ __ __ __ __

Not hello = <u>G</u> <u>O</u> __ __ __ __ __

A cart = __ __ <u>G</u> <u>O</u> __

Fairy-tale lizard = __ __ __ <u>G</u> <u>O</u> __

Didn't remember = __ __ __ <u>G</u> <u>O</u> __

Western state = __ __ __ <u>G</u> <u>O</u> __

Spanish friend = __ __ __ <u>G</u> <u>O</u>

City in Illinois = __ __ __ __ <u>G</u> <u>O</u>

BYE	LD	N
N	AMI	CA
N	LE	BB
FOR	RIL	DRA
LA	T	CHI
ORE	OD	WA

EXTRA FUN: These mini cars are racing across the page as fast as they can. How quickly can you circle the two that are exactly alike?

Super Fast Track

Of all the NASCAR tracks, on which one do the cars go the fastest? The answer is hidden in this pattern. Can you figure out how to read it?

Broken Record

Sometimes it's almost impossible to go slowly! Break the Last-to-First Code to learn how one racecar driver made this work for him!

ellT su arioM, owh idd ouy og os astf ni het astl acer?

yM rakesb on'td orkw. I antedw ot inishf eforeb I adh a rashc!

The King

The driver nicknamed "The King" is in the International Motorsports Hall of Fame and has also been named one of NASCAR's fifty greatest drivers. Over his thirty-five-year career he won a record 200 races. This includes winning twenty-seven races in just one season—ten of them in a row! So, who is "The King"? To find out, fit all the words into the grid. Then take the shaded letters and place them in order on the dotted lines. We left you T-H-E K-I-N-G to help you out!

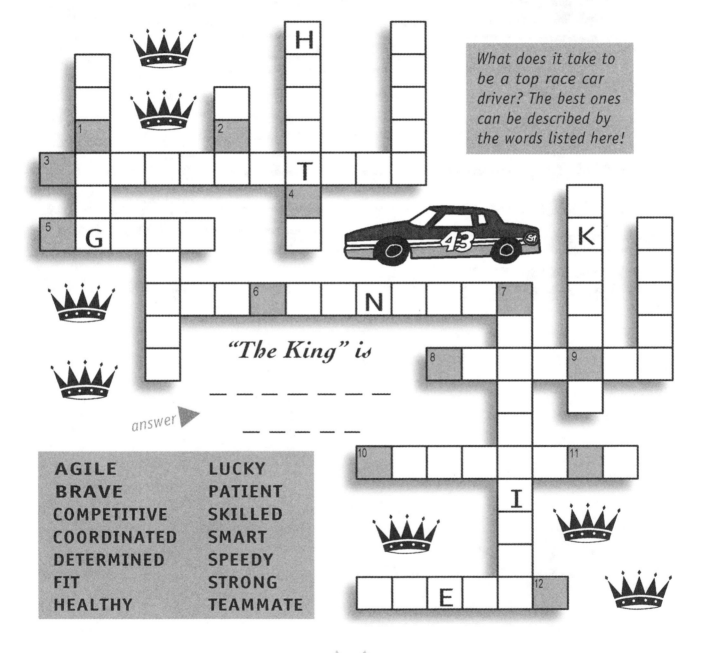

What does it take to be a top race car driver? The best ones can be described by the words listed here!

"The King" is

_ _ _ _ _ _

answer ▶

_ _ _ _ _ _

AGILE
BRAVE
COMPETITIVE
COORDINATED
DETERMINED
FIT
HEALTHY

LUCKY
PATIENT
SKILLED
SMART
SPEEDY
STRONG
TEAMMATE

Rough Rally

The longest road rally ever was one that started from Covent Garden, London, on August 14, 1977, and finished at the Sydney Opera House, Australia, on September 28, more than a month later! How many miles did the race cover? Solve the equations in each column, then read the five-digit number across the bottom.

6	10	7	4	2
+7	+2	-3	+9	+7
+1	-7	+6	-6	+10
-9	+9	-2	+4	-5
+3	-3	+6	-5	+1
-7	-2	-11	-4	-6
		,		

Lady Leader

A woman made history in 2005 when she led the Indianapolis 500. She led three times for nineteen laps and finished in fourth place—the best finish by a woman in the ninety-four years of the event! Who was she? Solve the picture equations to spell out her name.

first name

-PAN + 5 cents -KEL + -PPLE

last name

-CH + -NG + -TRU

BULLS-EYE BROTHERS

Only once in history have two brothers each won the championship of NASCAR's top series. Follow the directions to find out their last name.

1. Each clue suggests a five-letter word ending with N.
2. Write each word into the puzzle. Put the first letter in the outer ring and spell toward the middle.
3. Read the letters in the outer ring. Start with number 1 and read counterclockwise.

1. **Sour yellow fruit**
2. **Once more**
3. **To start**
4. **The sea**
5. **Strong fabric made from chemicals**
6. **Choo-choo**
7. **Consumed by mouth**

I am
OBYBB!

I am
YERTR!

EXTRA FUN:
Unscramble the brothers' first names!

First Place

Usually the spotlight is on winning drivers. But what about the cars? Over the years, what brand of car has won the most Formula One races? To find out, use the clues to fill in the puffs of exhaust. The last letter of one word is the first letter of the next. When you have finished, write the letters from the dark puffs on the dotted lines. Hint: Fill the puffs in order, even if it looks like you are spelling backward!

1. **Front part of the head where your eyes and nose are**
2. **A mistake**
3. **What a lion says**
4. **Part of the eye that sends messages to the brain**
5. **Opposite of before**
6. **Pasta stuffed with cheese**

What car maker creates the winning-est Formula One cars?

___ ___ ___ ___ ___ ___ ___

So Fast, So Young

This NASCAR star has been winning car races since he was a boy. He won his first quarter-midget car championship at age eight, and at age sixteen he was the youngest person ever granted a racing license by the United States Auto Club. Currently, he is a four-time NASCAR Cup Series champion. Who is he? To find out, fill in all the shapes with the letters F-A-S-T.

No, Thank You!

Katherine Legge is an up-and-coming Champ Car World Series driver. While she has won awards for both speed and driving ability, there is one award that Catherine wishes she hadn't won! Break the Upside-Down Flip-Flop Code to learn what it was.

[Upside-Down Flip-Flop coded message, handwritten]

FASTEST DRAG

Anthony Schumacher set a record for the fastest speed in a drag race in May 2005. He ended a 440-yard run going...well, to see just how fast he was going, fill in all the boxes with a horizontal line in the middle!

MILES PER HOUR

Indy Winners

Young and old drivers alike have won the Indianapolis 500. But wait a minute—these two champions have crashed into each other! See if you can untangle the letters to find out who the youngest and oldest Indy winners are! Hint: Use a light color marker to highlight one set of letters.

```
T t H h E e Y o O l U
N d G e E s S t T w W
I i N n N n E e R r I
S i T s R a O l Y u R
U n T s T e M r A w N
W h H o O w W a A s S
2 4 2 7 Y y E e A a R
S r A s N a D n 8 d O
D 3 A 6 Y O S d O a L
D y W s H o E l N d H
E w W h O e N n I h N
1 e 9 w 5 o 2 n . i X
X n X 1 X 9 X 8 X 7 X
X . X x X x X x X x X
```

Tough to Beat

Of all the auto races in the world, the Le Mans race in France is one of the most famous, and most famously difficult to win. The race goes for twenty-four hours straight—day and night, through heat, wind, or rain. The car that wins isn't always the one that comes in first, but the one that can cover the most miles in the twenty-four hours. That's why drivers have been known to speed over 250 miles per hour on the straight parts of the course! The teams of drivers who compete have a saying that shows just how tough they find this race. Use the decoder to see how fast you can figure out what they say!

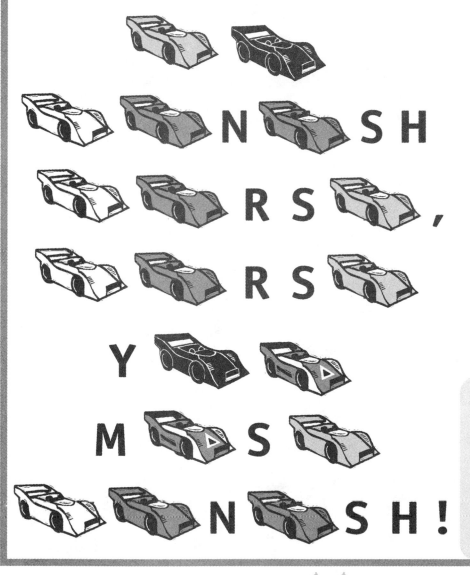

= F
= I
= O
= T
= U

Mega Wins

NASCAR driver Tony Stewart holds the record for the most money won in a single season. To learn how much he made in 2005, find your way through the maze from START to FINISH. Add up the numbers you can get to from the correct path and you will see just how successful Tony was that year. Write your answer in the money bag!

CHAPTER 9:
CRAZY CARS

Way to Go!

This motorsport started in California in the 1950s and was designed to be affordable family fun. Even kids as young as five years old could enjoy the thrill of driving these tiny cars! These days there are special tracks and zippy engines that can shoot these tiny cars along at up to 90 miles per hour. This sport now has loyal fans around the world. There are even plans to start racing a new generation of nonpolluting cars powered by fuel cells (hydrogen) instead of gasoline! What is the name of this sport that helped the likes of Michael Schumacher, Darrell Waltrip, Sam Hornish, Jr., Tony Stewart, Danica Patrick, and Kyle Petty get their racing start? Connect the dots in order from 1 to 63 and you will find out!

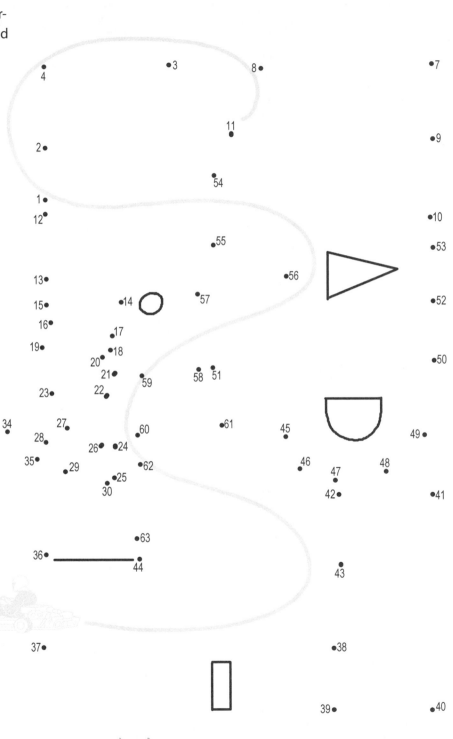

WHAT ARE THEY?

These crazy cars have absolutely massive engines that stick way out in front. The engines power huge wheels that stick way up in the back. They look like someone took a stock car, tilted it forward, gave it a wild paint job, and then sent it smokin' down the track! What kind of racecars are these? Color in everything but the ! ? / and * to find out!

!"!*F/?/U*!N/?N*!Y?C*
A!/R?S/!"A*R/!E*A?/K
!!N?/D?O?F?/D?R!/*
A*G?/R*A/?*C!/E?/R!?

Crazy Talk

These cars have started to speak their own crazy language! Can you break the code and figure out what they are laughing about?

"WZOOMHZOOMEZOOMRZOOMEZOOM
DZOOMOZOOM   RZOOMAZOOMCZOOMEZOOM
CZOOMAZOOMRZOOMSZOOM   GZOOMOZOOM
SZOOMWZOOMIZOOMMZOOMMZOOMIZOOMNZOOMGZOOM?"

"IZOOMNZOOM   TZOOMHZOOMEZOOM
CZOOMAZOOMRZOOM
PZOOMOZOOMOZOOMLZOOM!"

More Crazy Talk

Funny cars and top fuel dragsters are similar, but each of these racecars has a different nickname. To learn what they are, find the extra capital letters in each statement below. Put the first one in the space to the left and the second one to the right!

Funny Car nickname ▼

Top Fuel nickname ▼

Both are proFessional classes of Drag racing.
Both use racing aLcohol to fuel theIr cars.
BOth races Get started from a complete stop.
Both cars can hit sPeeds Greater than 325mph.
Both sPeed down a quartEr-mile racetrack.
Both racEs only take seconds to Run.
Both races aRe extremely noisy.

The Future Is Here!

In 2007, a car representing seven years of research and design by NASCAR will debut in the Nextel Cup Series. Everyone hopes that this car will improve the future of racing in three important areas: safety, performance, and the ability of race teams to control costs. That's just about everything!

What's the name of this wonder car? To find out, make a three-letter word in each column by placing a letter in the empty middle box. Choose from the letters underneath each grid. The words you make will read from top to bottom. When you are done, read across the shaded rows from left to right.

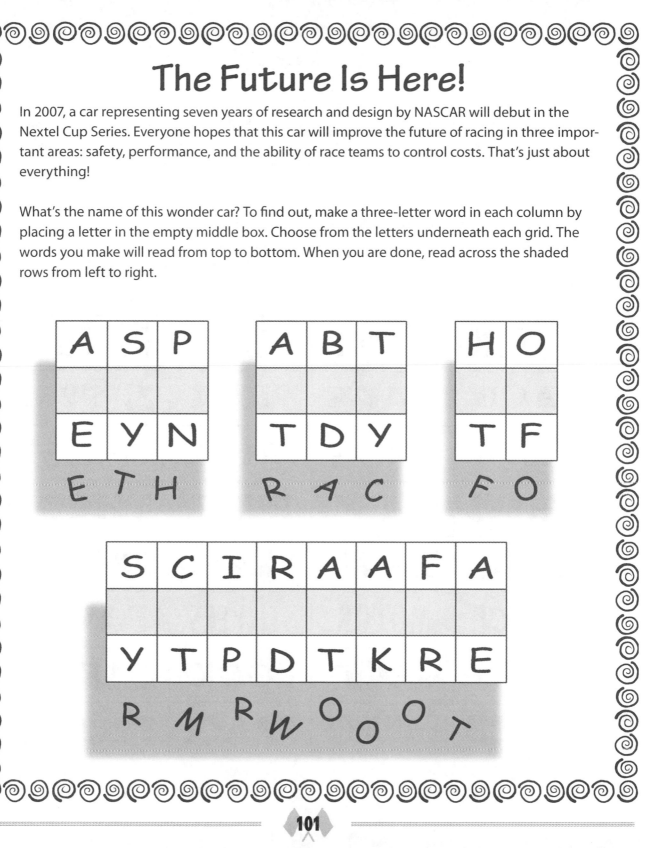

REALLY?

A high-tech stock racing car can cost more than $125,000 to build, but it is designed to look like a regular street car. However, one part of these cars only looks normal until you get up close. Then you see that this part is totally fake! What is it? Follow the directions to cross words out of the puzzle grid. Read the remaining words from left to right and top to bottom to learn about this crazy car part.

Cross out all the words that...rhyme with RACE
...mean the same as FAST
...are car parts with 5 letters

QUICK	STOCK	TIRES	RACE
PACE	CARS	PLACE	ZIPPY
DON'T	DASH	HAVE	CHASE
WHEEL	HEADLIGHTS	RUSH	THEY
ONLY	HAVE	TRACE	BRAKE
GRACE	MOTOR	STICKERS	FACE
THAT	RAPID	LOOK	LIKE
SPEED	HEADLIGHTS	SPACE	TRUNK

Scary Car

Each of the clues below suggests a word. Write the word on the dotted lines. Then put the letters in their proper place in the grid. Work back and forth between the grid and the clues until you have the crazy answer to the riddle!

Which kind of snakes are found on racecars?

A. To rip up = $\underset{16}{\_}\ \underset{6}{\_}\ \underset{15}{\_}\ \underset{8}{\_}\ \underset{10}{\_}$

B. Not tame = $\underset{1}{\_}\ \underset{12}{\_}\ \underset{9}{\_}\ \underset{4}{\_}$

C. Climbing plant = $\underset{11}{\_}\ \underset{2}{\_}\ \underset{3}{\_}\ \underset{14}{\_}$

D. Taste a drink = $\underset{5}{\_}\ \underset{7}{\_}\ \underset{13}{\_}$

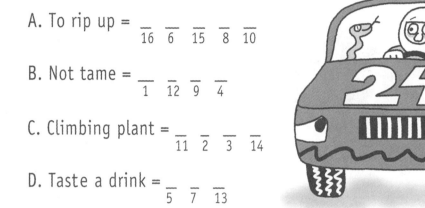

1B	2C	3C	4B	5D	6A	7D	8A	9B	10A
		11C	12B	13D	14C	15A	16A		

Who Is Driving?

If frogs could drive, what kind of racecars would they choose? Crack the frog code to find out!

OPH
ODSR

Mixed-up Mess

Whoa! All these different racecars have gotten jumbled up together.
First identify each numbered car on the list. Then answer the following
questions:

—Are there more pinewood derby cars or Vintage Formula One cars?

—There is only one of which kind of vehicle?

—If each car has four tires, how many tires are there altogether?

1. **Indy Car**
2. **Stock Car**
3. **Junior Dragster**
4. **Pinewood Derby Car**
5. **Slot Car**
6. **Vintage** Formula 1 Car
7. **Kart**

The New Kid

In 2007, a certain car manufacturer is joining the likes of Ford, Dodge, and Chevrolet in launching two new racing teams. Who is this newcomer to NASCAR? To find out, you will need to put one letter from the list into each empty box. This will make a familiar racing word that reads from left to right. The tricky part is that the empty box might be at the beginning, the middle, or the end of the mystery word!

When you are done, read down the shaded boxes to discover the answer. Caution: Some of the rows have extra letters that you don't need!

answer reads down

mystery words read across ▶

R	P	I		D	A	S
L	O	G		M	O	T
S	W	A		B	A	R
S	A	T		W	E	R
B	I	L		U	R	N
U	T	R		C	K	E

Y T A O T

Car Creations

Since 1953, Cub Scouts across the country have been creating and racing their own pinewood derby cars. These small, carved wooden cars run on gravity and can be painted to look like just about anything! Grab your markers, colored pencils, or crayons and decorate each blank car so it becomes a crazy racer! Hint: Look at the words scattered around the pages for ideas.

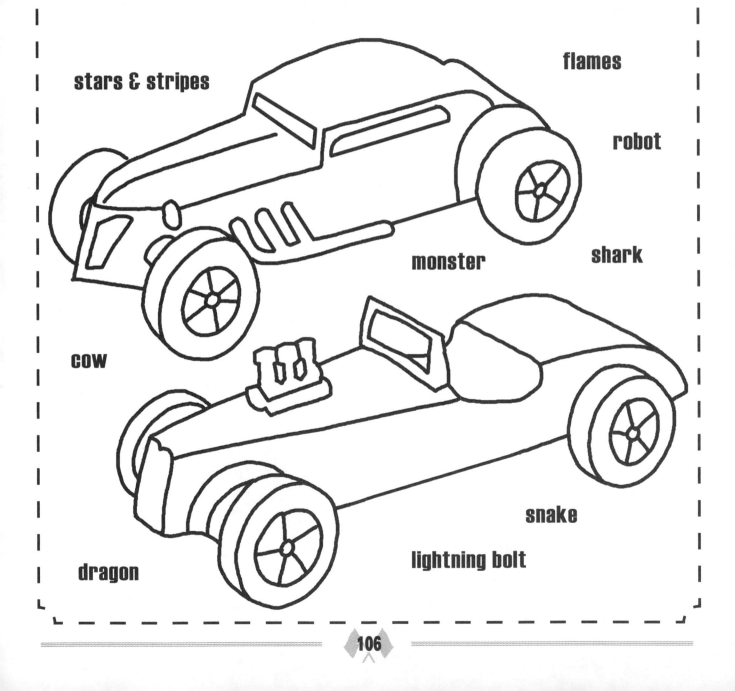

stars & stripes

flames

robot

shark

monster

cow

snake

lightning bolt

dragon

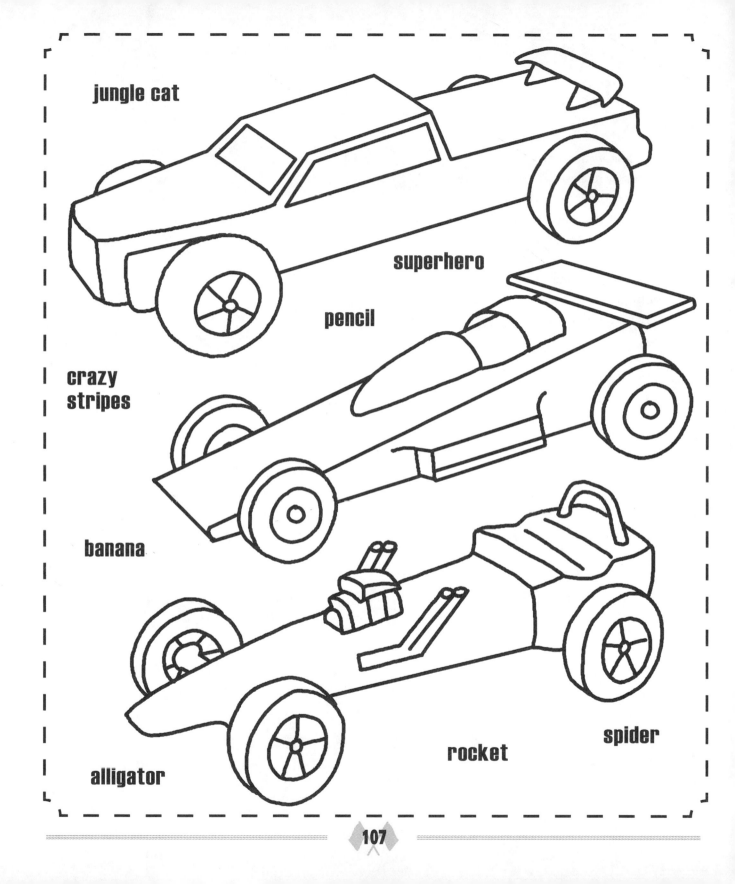

jungle cat

superhero

pencil

crazy
stripes

banana

alligator

rocket

spider

Extreme Gravity Racing

Student engineers at some colleges have the opportunity to design and build their own high-tech, gravity-powered race-cars. They meet at challenges to see which cars perform best on sharp turns and steep straightaways while reaching speeds up to 50 miles per hour. This is like a super soap box derby of the future!

Which route did this race-car take down the hill? The numbers on the correct path add up to 350, which is the allowable weight for an extreme gravity racing car plus driver.

START

20   40   50

50

20

25

50

60

20

10

40

20

20

20

20

70

30

20

25

10

25

30

10

10

30

10   10   20   10

Caution: Gravity-powered racecars can only travel on paths that lead down or across the hill!

Look Again!

Just when you thought the race was over, there are more puzzles to chase down! See if you can spot each of these picture pieces somewhere in this book. Write the name of the puzzle each piece is from in the space under each box. Hint: There is only one picture piece from each chapter!

1.

2.

3.

4.

5.

6.

7.

8.

9.

APPENDIX B: RESOURCES

If this puzzle book has inspired you to find out more about auto racing, we've provided you with some Web sites where you can get up-to-the-minute information on your favorite type of racing. In addition, we've suggested a couple of books and a film for your reading and viewing pleasure. Enjoy!

WEB SITES

www.nascar.com

The official site for everything NASCAR. Includes information on drivers, statistics, race-by-race standings, schedules, and video clips and sound bites of your favorite racing personalities. For up-to-the-minute news, this is the place to look.

www.formula1.com

The official site for Formula One racing. Offers the latest headlines, team and driver profiles and lineups, a Hall of Fame, and a photo gallery. Also includes an interactive circuit map for the different racetracks where they will be racing.

www.nhra.com

The official site of the National Hot Rod Association. It offers everything you want to know about drag racing. Topics covered range from A Day at the Drags to Driver Profiles and Blogs to Top News Stories.

www.danicapatrick.com

The official site of Indy Car driver Danica Patrick, the first woman ever to lead in the Indianapolis 500. A visually slick site featuring news articles, photographs, a personal journal, sponsor information, and even an online store for fans. Great music, too!

www.aasbd.com

The site for the All-American Soap Box Derby, a youth racing program that has run nationally since 1934.

Clearly explains what soap box derby is, details its history with photos, and tells you how you can get started—including a frequently asked questions section.

www.howstuffworks.com

A great site for finding out how just about anything works. If you search for "NASCAR," you'll find fascinating information including facts such as the headlights on racecars are really stickers! There are related articles as well on topics like safety and how NASCAR engines are different from street engines.

BOOKS

Racecar Alphabet, by Brian Floca (2004)

A thoughtfully planned picture book for kids of all ages—and their parents, too! It is a large-scale, beautifully illustrated A-Z tribute to the sport of auto racing, spanning time and types of racecars.

Eyewitness: NASCAR, by James Buckley (2005)

An overview of NASCAR from its birth to 2005. It has eye-catching photographs throughout and tons of details about the cars, drivers, races, and fans that make the sport great.

FILM

Cars (2006)

A Disney-Pixar animated film perfect for the entire family! Cleverly written, this humorous story of a rookie racecar is full of racing personalities and situations that race fans will certainly recognize. The real "King" himself, Richard Petty, provides the voice of Car #43, The King! Other guest appearances include racing greats Mario Andretti, Darrell Waltrip, Michael Schumacher, and Dale Earnhardt, Jr.

APPENDIX C: PUZZLE SOLUTIONS

Page vi • *Intro Answer*

Page 3 • *Chop Shop*

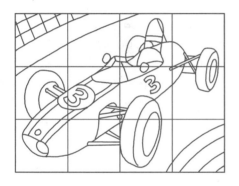

Page 4 • *Muscle Car*

Page 2 • *Slow and Steady*

10
miles per hour

Page 2 • *Number One*

Page 5 • *Big Changes*

1. Last 3/5 of MOTEL
2. First 2/5 of EVENT
3. Last 2/7 of CHASSIS
4. Last 1/2 of ACTION

T	E	L	E	V	I	S	I	O	N

1. First 1/2 of SPORTY
2. Middle 1/5 of LANES
3. Last 3/5 of VISOR
4. Middle 1/3 of DASHES
5. Last 3/5 of FLIPS

S	P	O	N	S	O	R	S	H	I	P	S

Page 6 • *Down and Dirty*

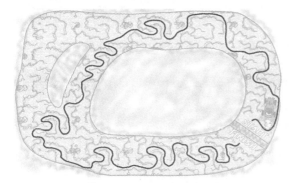

Page 6 • *Racing Is Born*

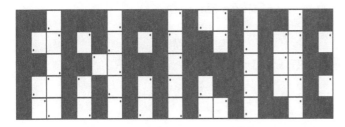

Page 7 • *Silly Speedster*

1G I	2A T		3G N	4B E	5C V	6H E	7F R
		8C G	9E O	10G E	11C S		
12F A	13A N	14H Y	15H W	16B H	17E E	18H R	19C E
20G W	21F I	22E T	23D H	24C O	25D U	26B T	
27H A		28B R	29A A	30D T	31E T	32C L	33B E

A. Light brown
$\underline{T}_{2}\ \underline{A}_{29}\ \underline{N}_{13}$

B. Number after two
$\underline{T}_{26}\ \underline{H}_{16}\ \underline{R}_{28}\ \underline{E}_{4}\ \underline{E}_{33}$

C. Clothing for hands
$\underline{G}_{8}\ \underline{L}_{32}\ \underline{O}_{24}\ \underline{V}_{5}\ \underline{E}_{19}\ \underline{S}_{11}$

D. Small shack
$\underline{H}_{23}\ \underline{U}_{25}\ \underline{T}_{30}$

E. To carry or haul
$\underline{T}_{31}\ \underline{O}_{9}\ \underline{T}_{22}\ \underline{E}_{17}$

F. What we breathe
$\underline{A}_{12}\ \underline{I}_{21}\ \underline{R}_{7}$

G. Drink from grapes
$\underline{W}_{20}\ \underline{I}_{1}\ \underline{N}_{3}\ \underline{E}_{10}$

H. Very tired
$\underline{W}_{15}\ \underline{E}_{6}\ \underline{A}_{27}\ \underline{R}_{18}\ \underline{Y}_{14}$

Page 9 • *That's a Race?*

First-to-Last Code
Umpire was required to ride in car to prevent cheating.

Vowel Scramble Code
Average speed was just over seven miles per hour.

Letter Switch Code
(A=B, B=C, C=D, etc.)
It took more than ten hours to travel 54 miles.

AEIOU/12345 Code
Waited for four minutes at a railroad crossing for train to pass.

Reverse Word Code
Had to find blacksmith shop to repair broken steering arm.

Page 8 • *Making Fast Cars*

Add the opposite of stop — PEU**GE**O**T**
Add quadruple Es and a Z — M**E**RC**E**D**E**S-B**E**NZ
Add a large rodent — **R**EN**A**UL**T**
Add the last two letters of HAT — F**I**A**T**
Add a place for cows — ALF**A** ROM**E**O
Add a place to sit — MA**SS**ER**A**T**I**
Add an insect — **B**UG**A**TTI
Add money to join a group — **D**UE**S**ENBERG
Add not feeling well — M**I**LLER
Add how old you are — DEL**A**G**E**
Add a delivery truck — **VAN**WALL
Add what you hear with — F**E**RR**A**R**I**
Add a policeman — **COP**ER
Add you and me — LOT**US**
Add a female horse — MCL**A**R**E**N
Add a writing tool — **PEN**SKE

Page 10 • *Try Hard*

Page 10 • *Zap*

W+2 = Y
V-2 = T
H+1 = I
B+1 = C
K-2 = I
Q+1 = R
U-1 = T
F-3 = C
B+3 = E
K+1 = L
I-4 = E

↳ Oops, we forgot to say read this from bottom to top!

Page 11 • *Mad Dash*

(road on the left)
BOOTLEGGING
——————————
RUMRUNNING
(road on the right)

Page 14 • *Fully Equipped*

Page 12 • *Founding Father*

NASCAR

Page 14 • *Oil Change*

COIL and TOIL (*change the I to* <u>O</u>) CO<u>O</u>L and TO<u>O</u>L

BOIL and SOIL (*change the O to* <u>A</u>) B<u>A</u>IL and S<u>A</u>IL

FOIL and COIL (*change the I to* <u>A</u>) FO<u>A</u>L and CO<u>A</u>L

Page 15 • *Bye Bye*

<u>T</u>HIR<u>T</u>Y <u>S</u>ECOND<u>S</u>!

Page 15 • *Quick Fix*

1. "Jerry, find Jeff a new jacket and helmet!"
2. "Ricky, donuts and coffee, PRONTO!"
3. "Bob, rake the soil off the track!"
4. "This is no time for fun, Nelson!"
5. "J.R.! A 'G' size bulb, and hurry!"
6. "What a snafu! Eleven broken pins!"
7. "J.B., ol' T.S. here needs a battery, NOW!"

Page 16 • *Racecar*

T<u>ER</u>RACE
CAR<u>PET</u>
EM<u>B</u>RACE
CAR<u>AMEL</u>
<u>G</u>RACE
<u>BOX</u>CAR
<u>B</u>RACE<u>LET</u>
CAR<u>NIVAL</u>
<u>T</u>RACE<u>S</u>
<u>S</u>CAR<u>F</u>
RACE<u>TRACK</u>
<u>S</u>CARE<u>CROW</u>
<u>B</u>RACE<u>S</u>
CAR<u>DBOARD</u>

Page 17 • *Ready...Set...Search*

```
P T T S T O P
I T O T O P I
T P S O S O T
S O P P T T S
T S I S O S O
T I S P I T P
O S T O P I T
P T O T I P O
I T N S T P P
P I T S O O P
```

Page 17 • *Zzzzz*

IT MAKES

THEM

EXHAUSTED

Page 18 • *Ouch*

$$\underline{A}_{1} \quad \underline{F}_{2}\underline{U}_{3}\underline{E}_{4}\underline{L}_{5}$$

$$\underline{I}_{6}\underline{N}_{7}\underline{J}_{8}\underline{E}_{9}\underline{C}_{10}\underline{T}_{11}\underline{I}_{12}\underline{O}_{13}\underline{N}_{14}!$$

Page 18 • *No, Really*

Race cars do not have fuel injectors. They only have carburators!

Page 19 • *Super Charged*

Page 20 • *Do The Hustle*

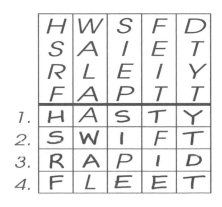

~~FOUR~~	THEY	~~74~~	~~43~~	CAN
DO	ALL	~~22~~	THAT	~~24~~
~~42~~	~~SEVEN~~	IN	~~TWO~~	AS
LITTLE	AS	~~34~~	15	~~72~~
~~47~~	~~28~~	OR	16	~~TWO~~
~~27~~	SECONDS	~~SEVEN~~	~~48~~	~~24~~

2 TIRE CHANGERS
2 TIRE CARRIERS
1 JACK MAN
1 GAS MAN
1 GAS CATCHER

HE GIVES THE DRIVER A DRINK!

SLAP
PALS
ALPS

The cars crossed the finish line in this order:
#24, #4, #6, #8

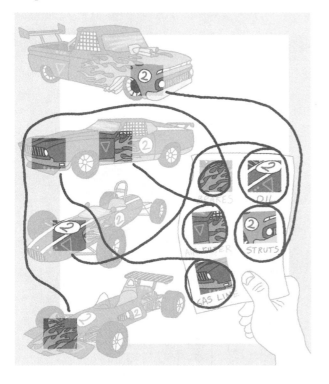

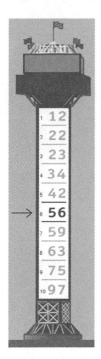

Page 28 • *Keeping Pace*

To run after = C H A S E

A location = P L A C E

The front of the head = F A C E

Area between things = S P A C E

Small bit left behind = T R A C E

Bottom of a mountain = B A S E

Event for fast cars = R A C E

Card worth most points = A C E

To hold steady = B R A C E

Prayer before dinner = G R A C E

Page 29 • *I Spy*

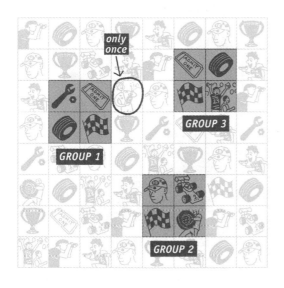

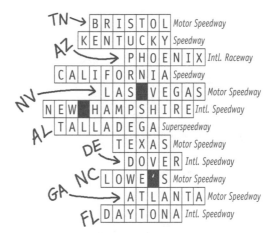

Page 33 • *Checkered Flag*

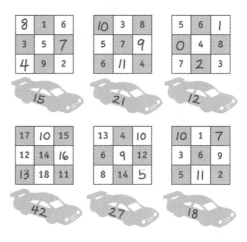

Page 36 • *Finish Line*

ON A ROAD COURSE DRIVERS MAKE BOTH LEFT AND RIGHTHAND TURNS

GREEN REGEN — start race	
YELLOW LOWYEL — caution	BLACK CLABK — penalty	RED DRE — stop
BLUE LUBE — passing	WHITE TIHEW — last lap	CHECKERED CREDCHEEK — end of race

	FINISH	LINE	
delete NI	FISH	NE	delete LI
add R in middle	FIRSH	ONE	add O to beginning
change H to T	FIRST	ONE ACROSS	add one more word that means "from one side to the other"

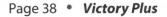

TEAR EDD SPOO SIXTHAY

Each winner also gets a
T R O P H Y

Possible Answers:
so, on, hi, is, son, sin, sip, hip, pin, hop, rip, pop, soon, hoop, ship, spin, poop, horn, spoon, snoop, shorn, hippo

QTPIE = *Cutie Pie*
10SNE1 = *Tennis anyone?*
4EVRL8 = *Forever Late*
1DRFUL = *Wonderful*
42N8 = *Fortunate*
A4DABL = *Affordable*
NVR1 = *Never Won*

XLR8
"accelerate"
to cause to move faster

Page 40 • *Get Me to the Race*

Page 41 • *Tons of Tires*

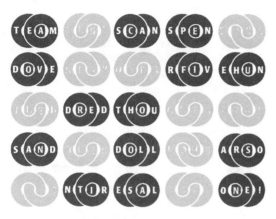

Teams can spend over five hundred
thousand dollars on tires alone!

Page 42 • *Hink Pinks*

C A S H   D A S H

B U C K   L U C K

R I C H   W I T C H

W I S E   P R I Z E

H O N E Y   M O N E Y

D O U G H   T H R O W

Page 44 • *Extra Fun*

10 - 5 - 6 - 6
J E F F
7 - 15 - 18 - 4 - 15 - 14
G O R D O N

Page 42 • *Crazy Money*

12 • 5 • 5 • 8 • 23
L E E H W
7 • 14 • 9 • 18 • 5 • 5 • 20 • 19
G N I R E E T S

Oops, forgot to mention that the answer is totally backwads!

Page 43 • *Many Sponsors*

$8,909,140

To break the code, hold the page up to a mirror. Then, move the last letter or number of each word to the beginning of the word.

Many teams own and operate several small planes. One owner, tired of keeping track of his 16 planes each race weekend, finally bought three 727 jets!

<u>Driver #1</u> = $10,000 (time trials)
   + $5,000 (headache) = $15,000

<u>Driver #2</u> = $50,000 (winning)
   + $4,000 (2 laps lead) = $54,000

<u>Driver #3</u> = $20,000 (sixth place) + $10,000 (front-runner)
   + $30,000 (15 laps led) = $60,000.

Answer: Driver #3 took home the biggest paycheck — more than the winner of the race!

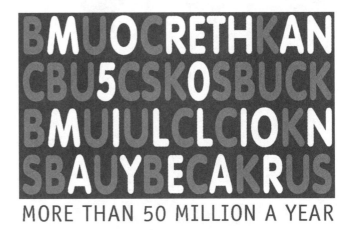

MORE THAN 50 MILLION A YEAR

answer ▼

A	S	K
C	A	T
I	L	L
P	A	D
A	R	E
H	I	P
B	E	D
U	S	E

answer ▼

O	W	E
B	I	G
O	N	E
I	N	K
$	I	N
A	N	D
E	G	G
A	S	H

answer ▼

P	E	N
I	N	N
A	D	D
M	O	M
E	R	S
A	S	E
$	E	A
E	M	U
B	E	E
A	N	T
I	T	$
U	S	E

different number 8

extra white stripe

other glasses are round

missing earplug

other watch is digital

stick longer

missing dot

should be letter B

missing color on stripe

word TICKET is reversed

F O R M U L A   O N E

Frantic Families Flap Festive Flags.

Crazy Couples Carry Cardboard Cutouts.

Wild Women Wave Wacky Wooden Wands.

Mischievous Men Make Monkey Moves.

Cheering Children Cast Colorful Confetti.

How do NASCAR drivers stay cool?

They sit close to the fans!

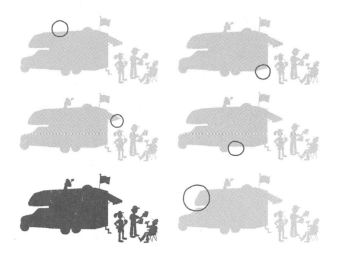

A long, pointed tooth = FAN **G**

Amazing! = FAN **T A S T I C**

An imaginative story = FAN **T A S Y**

Very decorated = FAN **C Y**

Rear end nickname = FAN **N Y**

Baby = **I N** FAN **T**

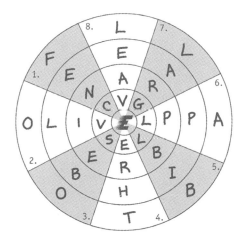

Page 57 • *Sign This, Please?*

| Matt Kenseth | Dale Earnhardt | Tony Stewart |
| Kevin Harvick | Rusty Wallace | Richard Petty |

Page 59 • *Traffic Jam*

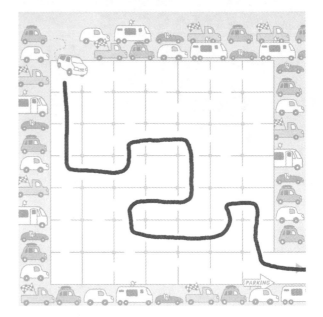

Page 58 • *Super Souvenirs*

```
L S A M A J A P R W A T C H D
E E T C G A L F D E C A L A O
W H I L S W E A T S H I R T L
O A L O S A L E E S O E S S L
T T F C L I K C E N I S O H E
D N A K S C O C A S R M C I E
C R H C A H O A O N D I K R S
A T E J E I B P S N O W S T O
L E L V E R T N I A H C Y E K
E N M U G W O B I V I S O R L
N T E L I D I E C A S T C A R
D O T R A D I N G C A R D N D
A S H E E T S O L M A G N E T
R L A R S S E S S A L G N U S
A Y P H O T O G R A P H E A R
```

Extra letters read: Retail sales of licensed NASCAR merchandise is now over two billion dollars a year!

Page 60 • *Wow!*

124

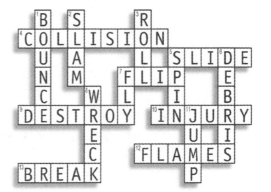

Page 63 • *Crazy Crash*

Driver #1: How did you manage to crash in the last race?

Driver #2: Did you see that big curve on the far side of the track?

Driver #1: Yes?

Driver #2: Well, I didn't!

Page 64 • *Sounds Bad*

The kill switch turns off a car's electrical power, or "kills" the engine, to slow the car down if the throttle gets stuck.

Page 64 • *Double Trouble*

Page 66 • *Draft Dodger*

The only car that didn't crash was car #2.

Page 65 • *Oh So Hot 2*

Page 65 • *Oh So Hot*

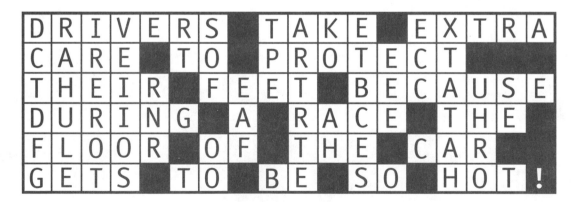

DRIVERS TAKE EXTRA CARE TO PROTECT THEIR FEET BECAUSE DURING A RACE THE FLOOR OF THE CAR GETS TO BE SO HOT!

START				
ROLL	OVER	SIDE	SHOW	TUNE
BACK	HAND	HILL	OFF	ROAD
STEP	MADE	UP	SCALE	WAY

END

1D R	2B E	3B S	4D T	5C R	6A I	7C C	8C T	9D O	10A R
	11A P	12B L	13C A	14A T	15C E	16B S			

A. To stumble
$\underset{14}{T} \underset{10}{R} \underset{6}{I} \underset{11}{P}$

B. Opposite of more
$\underset{12}{L} \underset{2}{E} \underset{16}{S} \underset{3}{S}$

C. Copy through thin paper
$\underset{8}{T} \underset{5}{R} \underset{13}{A} \underset{7}{C} \underset{15}{E}$

D. To decay
$\underset{1}{R} \underset{9}{O} \underset{4}{T}$

R+1 = S
O+5 = T
G-2 = E
C+2 = E
K+1 = L

Y+2 = A
R-4 = N
E-1 = D

H-2 = F
J+5 = O
Z+1 = A
I+4 = M

F-1 = E
Q-3 = N
B+3 = E
P+2 = R
J-3 = G
V+3 = Y

S-1 = R
A+4 = E
F-2 = D
T+1 = U
Z+3 = C
U-1 = T
G+2 = I
N+1 = O
S-5 = N

It was A WAD OF SOD

about eight inches
thick and two feet long!

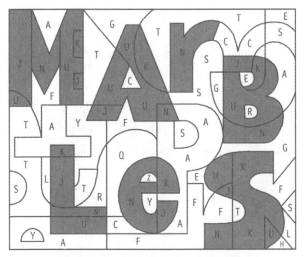

MARBLES

Part # 2

Part # 5

Part # 7

Part # 6

Part # 4

Part # 8

Part # 1

Part # 3

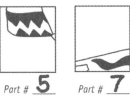

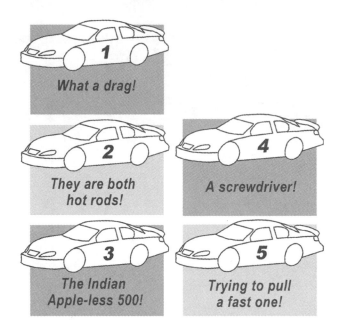

1 What a drag!

2 They are both hot rods!

4 A screwdriver!

3 The Indian Apple-less 500!

5 Trying to pull a fast one!

C LOT = *a lump of blood*

P I LOT = *person who flies a plane*

S LOT H = *slow, tree-hanging animal*

LOT I O N = *hand cream*

P LOT = *main story*

B A L LOT = *voting form*

LOT T E R Y = *a contest with numbered tickets*

O C E LOT = *small spotted wildcat*

C LOT H = *fabric*

B LOT = *spot or stain*

Car 1 has four vowels in its slot, and Car 2 has three vowels. Car 1 is the winner!

Page 79 • *Red Light, Green Light*

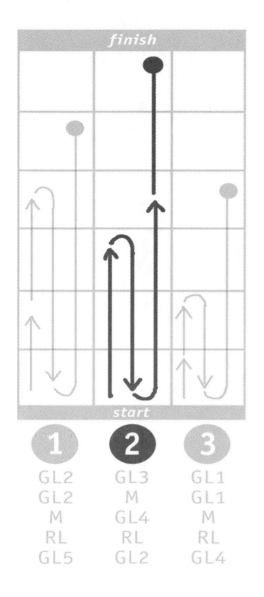

	1	2	3
	GL2	GL3	GL1
	GL2	M	GL1
	M	GL4	M
	RL	RL	RL
	GL5	GL2	GL4

Page 87 • *Broken Record*

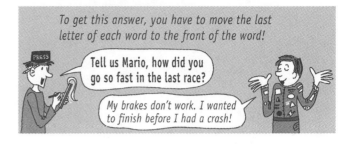

To get this answer, you have to move the last letter of each word to the front of the word!

Tell us Mario, how did you go so fast in the last race?

My brakes don't work. I wanted to finish before I had a crash!

Page 86 • *Fast as you Can*

Not silver = G O L D
Turkey noise = G O B B L E
Large ape = G O R I L L A
Not hello = G O O D B Y E
A cart = W A G O N
Fairy-tale lizard = D R A G O N
Didn't remember = F O R G O T
Western state = O R E G O N
Spanish friend = A M I G O
City in Illinois = C H I C A G O

Page 87 • *Super Fast Track*

To read this puzzle, you must turn the book one quarter turn clockwise. Now lift the book up to your chin, and tilt the top edge of the book away from you. You will now be looking up the long length of the letters. The further away you tilt the book, the shorter the letters appear. When you get the book in the right position, you will see that the letters spell "TALLADEGA." That's the answer!

Page 88 • *The King*

"The King" is
R I C H A R D
P E T T Y

Page 90 • *Bulls-eye Brothers*

I am Terry Labonte!

I am Bobby Labonte!

Page 89 • *Lady Leader*

first name

DA NIC A

last name

PAT RI CK

Page 91 • *First Place*

F E R R A R I

Page 89 • *Rough Rally*

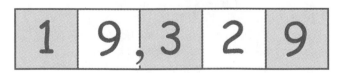

1 9,3 2 9

Page 93 • *Fastest Drag*

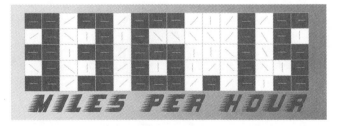

MILES PER HOUR

Page 92 • *So Fast, So Young*

Page 94 • *Indy Winners*

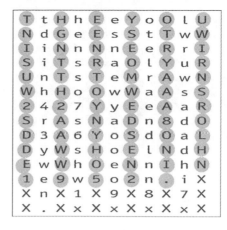

Page 93 • *No, Thank You!*

To read this code, you need to turn the page upside down in front of a mirror!

Katherine won the award for Biggest Hit of 2007 for her spectacular crash during a Champ Car Grand Prix. Even though her car was airborne, cartwheeled across the track, and landed upside down in pieces, Katherine walked away from the wreckage with just a few bruises. Amazing!

Page 93 • *Mega Wins*

Page 95 • *Tough to Beat*

TO FINISH FIRST, FIRST YOU MUST FINISH!

Page 98 • *Way to Go!*

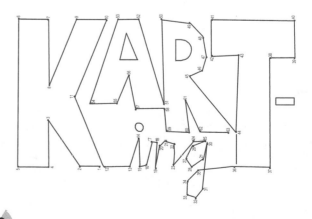

Page 99 • *What Are They?*

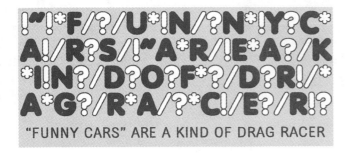

I"!*F/?/U*!N/?N*!Y?C*
A!/R?S/!"A*R/!E*A?/K
!IN?/D?O?F?/D?R!/*
A*G?/R*A/?*C!/E?/R!?

"FUNNY CARS" ARE A KIND OF DRAG RACER

Page 100 • *Crazy Talk*

To find the answer, cross out all the ZOOM words.

"Where do racecars go swimming?"

"In the car pool!"

Page 100 • *More Crazy Talk*

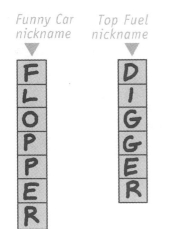

Funny Car nickname → F L O P P E R

Top Fuel nickname → D I G G E R

Page 101 • *The Future Is Here!*

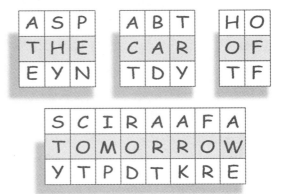

A	S	P
T	H	E
E	Y	N

A	B	T
C	A	R
T	D	Y

H	O
O	F
T	F

S	C	I	R	A	A	F	A
T	O	M	O	R	R	O	W
Y	T	P	D	T	K	R	E

Page 102 • *Really?*

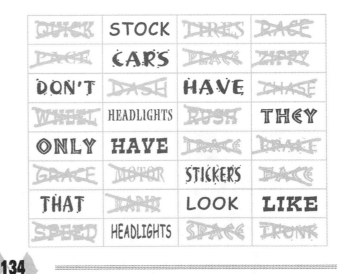

~~QUICK~~	STOCK	~~THREE~~	~~RACE~~
~~RACE~~	CARS	~~DRAG~~	~~ZIPPY~~
DON'T	~~DASH~~	HAVE	~~CHASE~~
~~WHEEL~~	HEADLIGHTS	~~RUSH~~	THEY
ONLY	HAVE	~~RACE~~	~~BRAKE~~
~~GRACE~~	~~MOTOR~~	STICKERS	~~RACE~~
THAT	~~DART~~	LOOK	LIKE
~~SPEED~~	HEADLIGHTS	~~SPACE~~	~~TRUNK~~

Page 103 • *Scary Car*

A. To rip up = $\underset{16}{S}\ \underset{6}{H}\ \underset{15}{R}\ \underset{8}{E}\ \underset{10}{D}$

B. Not tame = $\underset{1}{W}\ \underset{12}{I}\ \underset{9}{L}\ \underset{4}{D}$

C. Climbing plant = $\underset{11}{V}\ \underset{2}{I}\ \underset{3}{N}\ \underset{14}{E}$

D. Taste a drink = $\underset{5}{S}\ \underset{7}{I}\ \underset{13}{P}$

1B	2C	3C	4B	5D	6A	7D	8A	9B	10A
W	I	N	D	S	H	I	E	L	D

11C	12B	13D	14C	15A	16A
V	I	P	E	R	S

There are 18 pinewood derby cars and 19 slot cars.

There is only one vintage Formula One racecar.

There are 51 cars total. If each car has four tires, that makes 204 tires!

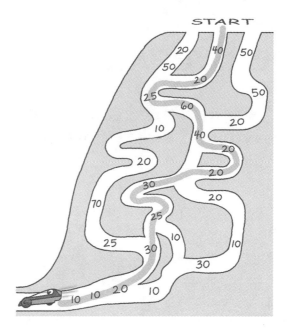

To get this answer, move the last letter of each word to the beginning of the word.

HOP RODS

1. Mad Dash   2. ZZZZZzzz   3. I Spy

4. Race Day, Payday   5. Feel Like a Fan   6. Crash Comments

7. Double Trouble   8. First Place   9. Scary Car

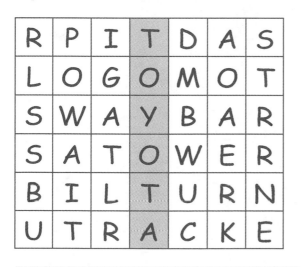

R	P	I	T	D	A	S
L	O	G	O	M	O	T
S	W	A	Y	B	A	R
S	A	T	O	W	E	R
B	I	L	T	U	R	N
U	T	R	A	C	K	E

The Everything® KIDS' Series!

Packed with tons of information, activities, and puzzles, the Everything® Kids' books are perennial bestsellers that keep kids active and engaged.

Each book is two-color, 8" x 9¼", and 144 pages.

The Everything® Kids' Fairies
Book
1-59869-394-8, $7.95

The Everything® Kids' Magical
Science Experiments Book
1-59869-426-X, $7.95

The Everything® Kids'
Environment Book
1-59869-670-X, $7.95

The Everything® Kids' Racecars
Puzzle and Activity Book
1-59869-243-7, $7.95

The Everything® Kids' Spies
Puzzle and Activity Book
1-59869-409-X, $7.95

A silly, goofy, and undeniably icky addition to the Everything® Kids' series . . .

The Everything® Kids'
GROSS
Series

Chock-full of sickening entertainment for hours of disgusting fun.

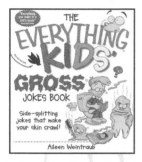

The Everything® Kids'
Gross Jokes Book
1-59337-448-8, $7.95

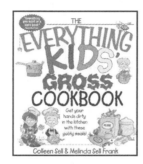

The Everything® Kids'
Gross Cookbook
1-59869-324-7, $7.95

The Everything® Kids' Gross
Puzzle & Activity Book
1-59337-447-X, $7.95

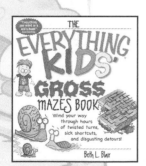

The Everything® Kids'
Gross Mazes Book
1-59337-616-2, $7.95

The Everything® Kids' Gross
Hidden Pictures Book
1-59337-615-4, $7.95

Other Everything® Kids' Titles Available

The Everything® Kids' Animal Puzzle & Activity Book
1-59337-305-8

The Everything® Kids' Baseball Book, 4th Ed.
1-59337-614-6

The Everything® Kids' Bible Trivia Book
1-59337-031-8

The Everything® Kids' Bugs Book
1-58062-892-3

The Everything® Kids' Cars and Trucks
Puzzle & Activity Book
1-59337-703-7

The Everything® Kids' Christmas Puzzle
& Activity Book
1-58062-965-2

The Everything® Kids' Cookbook
1-58062-658-0

The Everything® Kids' Crazy Puzzles Book
1-59337-361-9

The Everything® Kids' Dinosaurs Book
1-59337-360-0

The Everything® Kids' First Spanish Puzzle & Activity Book
1-59337-717-7

The Everything® Kids' Halloween Puzzle &
Activity Book
1-58062-959-8

The Everything® Kids' Hidden Pictures Book
1-59337-128-4

The Everything® Kids' Horses Book
1-59337-608-1

The Everything® Kids' Joke Book
1-58062-686-6

The Everything® Kids' Knock Knock Book
1-59337-127-6

The Everything® Kids' Learning Spanish Book
1-59337-716-9

The Everything® Kids' Math Puzzles Book
1-58062-773-0

The Everything® Kids' Mazes Book
1-58062-558-4

The Everything® Kids' Money Book
1-58062-685-8

The Everything® Kids' Nature Book
1-58062-684-X

The Everything® Kids' Pirates Puzzle and Activity Book
1-59337-607-3

The Everything® Kids' Presidents Book
1-59869-262-3

The Everything® Kids' Princess Puzzle & Activity Book
1-59337-704-5

The Everything® Kids' Puzzle Book
1-58062-687-4

The Everything® Kids' Riddles & Brain Teasers Book
1-59337-036-9

The Everything® Kids' Science Experiments Book
1-58062-557-6

The Everything® Kids' Sharks Book
1-59337-304-X

The Everything® Kids' Soccer Book
1-58062-642-4

The Everything® Kids' States Book
1-59869-263-1

The Everything® Kids' Travel Activity Book
1-58062-641-6

All titles are $6.95 or $7.95 unless otherwise noted.

Available wherever books are sold!
To order, call 800-258-0929, or visit us at *www.adamsmedia.com*
Everything® and everything.com® are registered trademarks of F+W Publications, Inc.
Prices subject to change without notice.